IMAGES
of America

MELROSE

VOLUME II

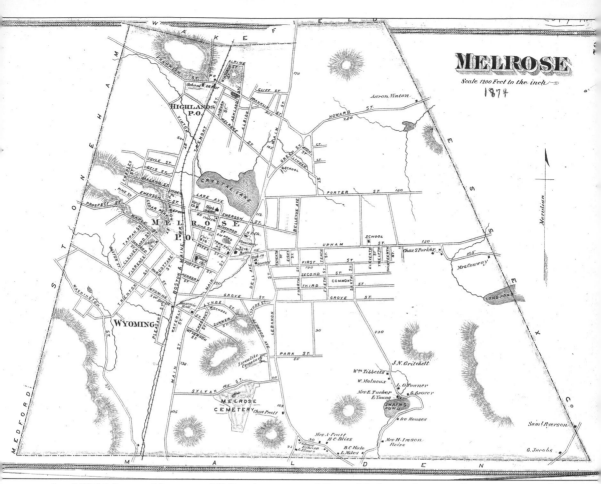

AN 1874 MAP OF MELROSE. Ell Pond was named Crystal Lake at the time this map was made. It was originally called Ell Pond, but its name was changed to Crystal Lake in the 1800s (it was later changed back to Ell Pond). Note Lake Avenue (adjacent to the pond) and the area's many brooks.

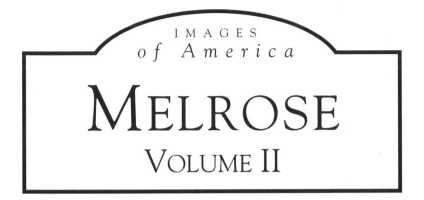

IMAGES
of America

MELROSE
VOLUME II

Anthony Pagano

ARCADIA

Published by Arcadia Publishing,
an imprint of Tempus Publishing, Inc.
2 Cumberland Street
Charleston, SC 29401

Printed in Great Britain.

Library of Congress Catalog Card Number: 98-87779

For all general information contact Arcadia Publishing at:
Telephone 843-853-2070
Fax 843-853-0044
E-Mail arcadia@charleston.net

For customer service and orders:
Toll-Free 1-888-313-BOOK

Visit us on the internet at http://www.arcadiaimages.com

CONTENTS

ACKNOWLEDGMENTS

I wish to thank the dedicated members of the Melrose Historical Society for their assistance, and the many people who shared their photographs and knowledge of Melrose with me. Of great help were Capt. John O'Brien of the Melrose Fire Department; Irene Conway, Melrose Historical Society; Edward Perkins, Melrose Historical Society; Marie Lingblom; Evelyn Parker; Elfrieda Scarborough; Mary MacDougall; Miriam H. Walsh, Melrose Historical Society; Bob Sherman; Jean Gorman, Director of C. of C.; Marie Wood; Dorothy Leary; Jane D'Allesandro, Reference Librarian, Melrose Public Library; Dennis J. Kelly, Director, Melrose Public Library; Priscilla and Herbert Gray; Eugene Garbati; Edward Dickie; Chief of Police Frank Fiandaca; Florence Bernard; Doug Christie; Eleanor Harris; Mary Marchant, Stoneham Historical Society; Mrs. Cremins; Mrs. James Umile; Mary and Catherine Sullivan; Carol McKinley, Melrose Historical Society; Ralph Sarni, President, Mt. Hood Park Association; Former Mayor James Milano; Ken Turino, Director, Lynn Historical Society; John Parziale; Joseph McKay; Rick Cantone; Jeff Luxenberg; Arnold Williams, Melrose Historical Commission; Edna Ford; Harold Poole; Mrs. K. Herrick; Mrs. Ball; Phil Cargill; John Ingersoll; Beth Gandelman; John Cinella; Mrs. A. Blades; William Minier; Mildred Baldwin; Dorothy Pearl; Churchill American Little League; Edna Ford; Elinor G. Laudin; Madeline Edmonds; Peter Regan; and Richard Amirault.

The various works I consulted in compiling this project include Elbridge H. Goss's *History of Melrose* (1902), Corey's *History of Malden* (1899), Edwin C. Kemp's *Melrose*, Melrose Historical Society's *Looking Back at Melrose*, Charles H. Adams's *Melrose "Town and City"* (1900), and Levi Gould and Franklin P. Shumway's *Ancient Melrose*. Also used in my research were the *Melrose Journal*, the *Melrose Free Press*, the *Boston Globe*, Middlesex South Registry of Deeds, the *Melrose Atlas*, Assessors Records, the *Melrose Reporter*, building permits, the Stoneham Historical Society, and the Melrose Historical Commission.

Foremost, many thanks to my wife, Mary, my co-partner as Oral Historians of the Melrose Historical Society. She has worked diligently along with me on this worthy project.

Many thanks to everyone who helped and are not listed.

TO ERR IS HUMAN—TO FORGIVE DIVINE

A BRIEF HISTORY

According to Goss's *History of Melrose*, in 1640 Thomas Coytmore built a dam and a gristmill at Black Rock, on the Mystic side of Three Myle Brook (Ell Pond Brook). In 1806, the Odiorne brothers maintained a firm which manufactured nails. Nearby, William Barrat operated a silk-dyeing business.

Three ponds were located in the Wyoming Cemetery. Now all have been eliminated. Dix Pond was located adjacent to Main Street, Melrose Square. Mr. Dix had a farm on the site of the city hall, which was built in 1874. The pond has vanished and now is the parking area in back of Memorial Hall and the fire station. At one time a brook flowed from Ell Pond to Dix Pond.

On Franklin Street, near the site of the Highland Congregational Church, was the Highland Pond and a brook which flowed to Ell Pond. Other ponds were Swains Pond, Towners Pond, Long Pond, and an assortment of brooks.

Envision yourself as an early settler from the town of Charlestown. About 1634–35 you boarded a boat to cross the Mystic River and landed at Sandy Bank (Malden) near the general location of what is now Medford Street Bridge and the Bell Rock Cemetery. The early inhabitants of Melrose are at rest in Bell Rock Cemetery, including Lieutenant Phineas Upham, born in 1635, who while fighting in King Philip's War was wounded at the Battle of Narragansett Fort, on December 19, 1675. He died of his wounds 10 months later in 1676, at the age of 41.

Assume you had recently constructed a house with the wood available from the surrounding forests. Your problems would soon multiply. Mr. Goss in his *History of Melrose* reminds us that in addition to disputes with Native Americans, our woods were alive with wild animals, deer, foxes, bears, wolf packs, and wild cats. The problems were severe and in 1630, 1635, and 1640, laws were passed by the colony authorities giving a bounty for the killing of wolves and foxes.

Mr. Woods, in the *New England Prospect*, speaks of the great annoyance of the wolves, rattlesnakes, mosquitoes, and black bears. The domestic animals needed protection. In the snowy winters the wild animals hung around the settlement in great packs and were feared by all. Deer would devour garden edibles unless the crops were suitably protected by fences.

Over the centuries, the settlers traveled the old Native-American trail from Malden Square, following what is now Mt. Vernon Street, Malden, over Mount Prospect (Waytes Mount) to the general area of the entrance of Malden's Forestdale Cemetery. Melrose's first settler received lots of land on the north side of Waytes Mount and gradually secured a great portion of the southern territory of Melrose.

In 1638, at the entrance of Forestdale Cemetery, Deacon Thomas Lynde constructed his first home in North Malden. In 1645, a second house was built at the old entrance of what is now Wyoming Cemetery on Sylvan Street, just south of Boston Rock. Apparently this was the first dwelling in Melrose. As proof, a remonstrance was recorded in the Massachusetts Archives, Vol. 121, p. 21, dated March 16, 1648, to form a committee to develop the Winnesimet (Chelsea) to Reading Road.

Accepted in 1653, the road winds through what is now Forestdale Cemetery, then through the rear of Pine Banks Park (then the Lynde family property). A portion of the narrow dirt road of 1653 still exists today; it continued into the old section of the Wyoming Cemetery to the cemetery entrance on Sylvan Street. From there it went to the westerly side of Boston Rock following the high ground near Main Street. The road was not improved and straightened until 1805.

The 1653 road joined Main Street in the vicinity of Mt. Vernon Street or via Linwood Avenue. At Lynde Street, the Reading Road twisted and turned following the high ground to Lebanon Street, avoiding small streams. From Lebanon Street the 1653 road continued to Main Street to Green Street and Main Street to Reading with slight deviations. As Deacon Thomas Lynde's family increased, a third dwelling was built in 1670 at 86 Main Street (now the site of Hunt Photo and NHD stores). It is believed the house was constructed for the deacon's son, Ensign Thomas Lynde. Around 1700 the home was altered and enlarged (there is a mural of the Lynde house on the wall of the Melrose Square office of MassBank). After several changes in ownership, the property was sold in 1956 and the house demolished in one day.

One

ABOUT THE TOWN OR CITY

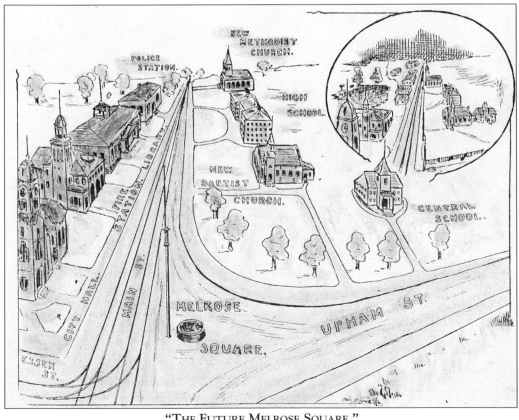

"THE FUTURE MELROSE SQUARE."

THE CORNER OF WAVERLY PLACE AND WEST WYOMING AVENUE. The house on the right has been replaced with an apartment and business building. Also, the trees are gone. Notice the elegant fence.

THE WIDENING OF MAIN STREET, LOOKING SOUTH TOWARD MELROSE SQUARE, 1892.

A Photo of 84 Cottage Street, Another of the 1848 Cottages. This home is a slight variation of 72 Cottage Street. The area was all farmland before these homes were built. On Independence Day, it was a short walk to the station to board the special trains of open freight cars to see the military display and fireworks. The railroad did not have enough passenger cars so if it rained, you came home soaking wet.

THE COLBY WING ADDITION TO THE MELROSE WAKEFIELD HOSPITAL. Generous patrons of the hospital, the Colbys gave the necessary funds for the addition.

Two
CHURCHES

A c. 1902 CARTOON IN THE *MELROSE FREE PRESS*. In the early days of the automobile, auto engines would frequently explode. A kerosene oil burner was recommended by this cartoon ad.

THE RUINS OF MELROSE ABBEY, SCOTLAND, BUILT ABOUT THE 14TH CENTURY. A support section was brought to Melrose and installed in the Trinity Episcopal Church on West Emerson Street in 1886. You have to look overhead to notice it.

DOWNTOWN MELROSE, SCOTLAND. Melrose, Massachusetts, took the name after a suggestion offered by Mr. Bogle, a native of Scotland.

TRINITY EPISCOPAL CHURCH. On April 13, 1856, 15 persons convened for church services at the home of Mr. and Mrs. Samuel Rice of 49 Lake Avenue with the Rev. W.H. Rice conducting. As the attendance increased, services were moved to the First Congregational Church, next to the Lyceum Hall on Main Street, for 18 months. From December 1857 to April 1860, services were conducted in Waverly Hall, at the corner of W. Emerson and Essex Streets across from the Melrose Train Depot. By 1860, a new church opened its doors for services. At a later occasion, a carved stone from the ruins of Melrose Abbey in Scotland was placed near a support on the front wall. In 1911, a parish house was constructed. It was destroyed by fire in 1936, but a larger parish house was erected within a year and enlarged in 1956.

THE FIRST UNITED METHODIST CHURCH OF MELROSE, 645 MAIN STREET. This, the first organized church in Melrose (then North Malden), was organized in 1813. In 1818, a meetinghouse was built at the corner of Main and Green Streets. A second church was built in 1857 on the present site, on land given by Isaac Emerson, and was destroyed by fire in 1903. The parishioners rallied to the cause and a new church was dedicated on June 19, 1904. The parish hall was built in 1925. Isaac Emerson's residence became the parsonage in 1861, and it was replaced in 1890 by the present home.

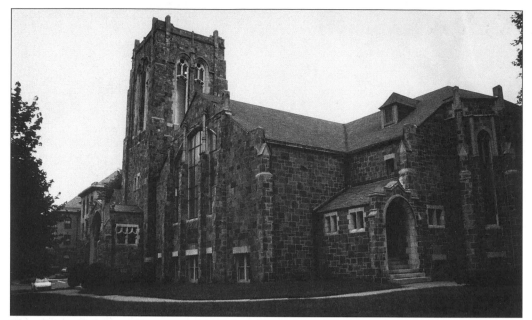

THE FIRST BAPTIST CHURCH, 561 MAIN STREET. In 1829, a small group of Methodist Episcopals left to form the Protestant Methodist Church. They bought the little district schoolhouse at the corner of Lebanon and Upham Streets and moved it to the corner of Main and Upham Streets. After enlarging it, a dedication took place in 1830. In 1842, a larger wooden church was erected. By 1845, the religious group was joined by several Baptists. The Baptists assumed financial responsibility and the First Baptist Church was organized on January 1, 1856. By the 1870s, the wooden church was sold to the Catholic Society and moved to Dell Avenue, near the corner of Upham Street. A new brick church was erected and dedicated November 17, 1874. With a rapid growth in membership, a new larger edifice was needed. With that need came the end of the Red church. (Bob Sherman.)

THE NEW CHURCH, DEDICATED APRIL 7, 1907. In 1954 a parish house was added for school rooms and a Fellowship Hall was constructed. The church was refurbished in 1981.

THE MELROSE HIGHLAND
CONGREGATIONAL CHURCH, 355
FRANKLIN STREET, REV. DR. RAND
PEABODY, INTERN PASTOR. On
September 29, 1875, 30 members
organized the Melrose Highlands
Congregational Church. A new
church was built at the corner of
Franklin and Ashland Streets, and
was dedicated September 29, 1880.
Due to rapid growth, a new building
became necessary. The old church
was sold to the Shepard Silver
Company and moved across the
street. In 1896, the church was
opened, but it was not until
December 5, 1919, that the debt was
declared free.

THE PRESENT APPEARANCE OF THE HIGHLAND CONGREGATIONAL CHURCH.

FAITH EVANGELICAL CHURCH, 200 FRANKLIN STREET, REV. DAVID SQUIRE, MINISTER.
This church began in 1900 as the Advent Christian Church. On April 12, 1912, the church bought the property of the Melrose Highlands Baptist Church on Franklin and Albion Streets. Today it is called Faith Evangelical Church.

TEMPLE BETH SHALOM, 21 E. FOSTER STREET, MELROSE. Services are held regularly.

ST. MARY OF THE ANNUNCIATION CHURCH ON THE CORNER OF HERBERT AND MYRTLE STREETS. This view does not show the high pointed spire, which was removed years ago. In 1891, the cornerstone of the church was set in place, with the dedication held in November 1893. The first pastor was the Reverend Francis J. Glynn. In 1895, the residence of Albert D. Holmes on Myrtle Street was purchased as a rectory (now demolished and used as a parking lot). In 1963, a new rectory was built across the street at 46 Myrtle Street.

THE FIRST CHURCH OF THE NAZARENE, 2 SHORT STREET, ON THE CORNER OF GREEN STREET, DONALD M. DAVIS, JR., PASTOR. The church was first organized August 26, 1928, by Rev. Howard V. Miller, district superintendent for New England, and Rev. K.M. Jackson, pastor of the Church of the Nazarene in Malden. In January 1930, services were held in the Boardman Block, Main Street. A new church was dedicated October 11, 1935. Renovations have changed the church, bringing it up to date.

A VIEW OF THE PRESENT CHURCH OF THE NAZARENE.

INCARNATION CHURCH, 429 UPHAM STREET, REV. D.F. DELANEY AND REV. L.E. PRATT, CO-PASTORS. This is one of the new churches in Melrose. It was created by dividing St. Mary's Parish lines in order to gain sufficient territory for the new parish. The church and parking area site were formerly the Kiley Farm.

CHURCH OF CHRIST, 409 UPHAM STREET, MARK WILSON, MINISTER. A modern-style church was recently built at 409 Upham Street, next door to the Incarnation Church property.

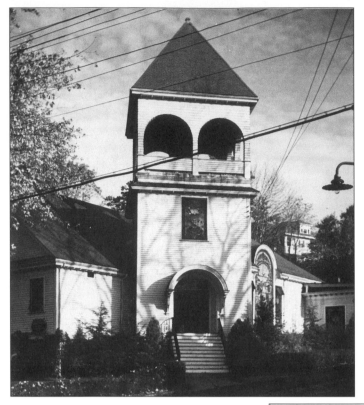

THE GREEN STREET BAPTIST CHURCH, 179 GREEN STREET, REV. LAWRENCE STARR, MINISTER. In 1893, Mrs. Emma J. Prince and Mr. George McCallum organized meetings which led to the development of a church society on February 5, 1894. In the same year, land was purchased at the corner of Green Street and Farwell Avenue. A church was partially started with the labor provided by many of its members. Since October 12, 1912, the church has been known as the Green Street Baptist Church. Land and a house used as a parsonage were purchased in 1928. In 1939, 1943, and 1947, renovations were completed.

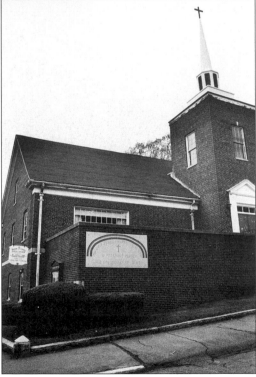

A PRESENT-DAY VIEW OF THE GREEN STREET BAPTIST CHURCH.

THE MELROSE UNITARIAN-UNIVERSALIST CHURCH, 70 W. EMERSON STREET, REV. PHYLLIS O'CONNELL. The First Unitarian service was held in 1848. Different locations served the church members until May 1, 1872, when a new church was dedicated. As the church membership grew in the 1930s, a desire for a new church was climaxed. Unfortunately, a generous benefactor, Frederick P. Bowden, did not live to see the completion. Mrs. Bowden aided with a special gift, resulting in an enlarged building by the dedication in 1956. The change took place in 1974, combining the Universal with the Unitarian Church, now the Melrose Unitarian-Universalist Church. (Bob Sherman.)

THE FIRST CHURCH OF CHRIST SCIENTIST AT 84 GREEN STREET, LYNN FELLS PARKWAY. The church was organized August 6, 1914. Meetings were held in Masonic Hall in 1925. By 1930, the cornerstone of the present church on Green Street and the nearby Lynn Fells Parkway was in place. It was ready for occupancy in November 1930, but was not dedicated until 1945, when the mortgage document was shredded.

THE VINEYARD CHRISTIAN FELLOWSHIP, 316 UPHAM STREET, MARK G. FEE, PASTOR. The Vineyard Christian Fellowship was previously the Hillcrest Congregational Church, begun in 1895. Meetings took place in the vacant Upham Hill School House, where a Sunday school was started. For the next two years, it was known as the East Side Mission. Later, in 1905, it became the East Side Chapel of the Congregational Church. In 1920, the chapel officially became the Hillcrest Church, and on June 1, 1924, the church was dedicated. It is now the Vineyard Christian Fellowship, 316 Upham Street.

THE FIRST CONGREGATIONAL CHURCH U.C.C., 121 W. FOSTER STREET, REV. THOMAS H. EVANS, MINISTER. The first service took place in the home of Dr. Levi Gould on Main Street, April 25, 1848. Other locations were used until the first church was built in 1849 on West Foster Street; in 1869 the church burnt down. A new church replaced the old, and was dedicated October 26, 1870. In 1882, a parsonage was added, and there have been many changes and additions since. On Thanksgiving evening, November 23, 1967, the church was destroyed by fire. Plans were formulated quickly and a new church was built in a modern style.

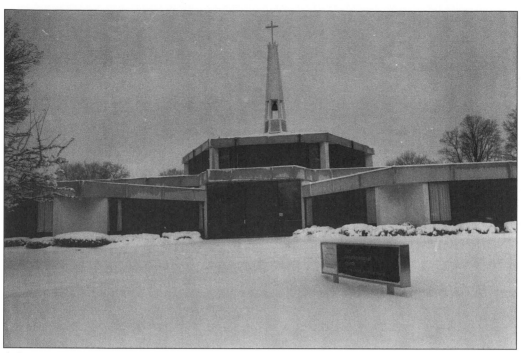

A VIEW OF THE NEW CONGREGATIONAL CHURCH. (Bob Sherman.)

PREPARING THE SITE OF THE TOWER PLAZA FOR THE FIRST NATIONAL STORES. This home was moved to another location. Today, Johnnie's Foodmaster and other stores are in the plaza.

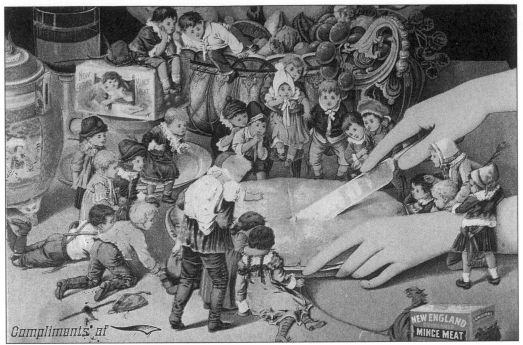

An Advertising Souvenir, Compliments of Frost & Hall, Fancy Grocers, Located in the Melrose Highlands. The grocers at one time had a store at the corner of Essex and Main Streets, in the Boardman Block.

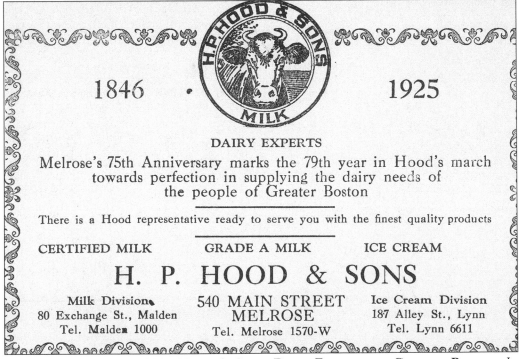

1846 · 1925

MILK

DAIRY EXPERTS

Melrose's 75th Anniversary marks the 79th year in Hood's march towards perfection in supplying the dairy needs of the people of Greater Boston

There is a Hood representative ready to serve you with the finest quality products

CERTIFIED MILK   GRADE A MILK   ICE CREAM

H. P. HOOD & SONS

Milk Division,
80 Exchange St., Malden
Tel. Malden 1000

540 MAIN STREET
MELROSE
Tel. Melrose 1570-W

Ice Cream Division
187 Alley St., Lynn
Tel. Lynn 6611

An Advertisement of H.P. Hood & Sons, Dairy Experts for Greater Boston. In 1925, Hood & Sons celebrated its 75th anniversary. The office was located at 540 Main Street.

Three
STREET SCENES

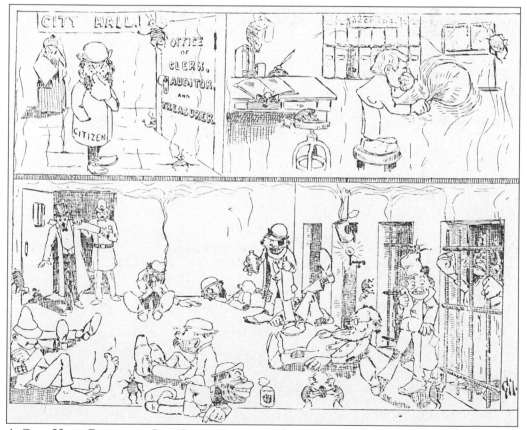

A CITY HALL BASEMENT JAIL SCENE. Intoxicated persons were housed in the basement jail. During the summer months odors arose to the first-floor offices, causing everyone to complain about the situation.

THE MELROSE HIGHLANDS RAILROAD STATION IN THE 1940S. It has been demolished.

THE SENIOR CHORUS LED BY SHARON CARTER. The chorus is shown here performing at the First Baptist Church for a senior citizens Christmas party.

THE FIRST OBSERVATION TOWER AT MT. HOOD PARK. The tower was installed by J.F. Slayton, and later burnt down. It was replaced in the 1930s by the Works Projects Administration (WPA).

THE MT. HOOD TOWER, REBUILT BY THE WPA IN 1935. (Marie Wood.)

THE SHEPARD MANUFACTURING COMPANY, 344 FRANKLIN STREET. The Shepard Manufacturing Company was founded by Chester Shepard and his son, Chester B. Shepard, for the manufacturing of high-grade sterling silverware and jewelry. They came from Middletown, Connecticut, where Chester Sr. worked for Middletown Silver Company, later absorbed by International Silver Company. The Shepards first started business in Melrose in 1891 in an old building at the rear of 153 West Emerson Street (this building was razed some years ago). In 1896, as business increased, they purchased the old Congregational wooden church, adjacent to the premises at 344 Franklin Street, which they altered and enlarged. The company prospered, manufacturing souvenir spoons marketed around the world.

TWO CHILDREN HAVING THEIR PICTURE TAKEN. In the background is the Melrose Chemical Company, on Essex Street, now part of the Deering Lumber Company.

MELROSE'S BIG BLAST, SEPTEMBER 21, 1904. A street trolley hit cases of dynamite lying in its path on Main Street at West Wyoming Avenue, causing an enormous explosion. In the darkness the motorman did not see the cases in the street and his body was hurled through the air. The trolley was a crumbled wreck. Nine people were killed and 40 hurt. Building fronts were damaged and glass windows blown out near the explosion. It was Melrose's worst local tragedy to that time. (Sketch by Neva Currey.)

BOWDEN PARK AS IT APPEARED YEARS AGO AT THE CORNER OF VINTON AND W. EMERSON STREETS. (Marie Wood.)

31

A VIEW OF THE SKI SLIDE AT MT. HOOD, BUILT BY THE WPA IN THE 1930S.

THE MORGAN & DODGE HOME FOR AGED WOMEN. The home was located on the corner of Cliff and Franklin Streets. In 1899, Miss Charlotte Morgan lived at 265 Franklin Street on a 21,000-square-foot lot equipped with sewerage and water lines. Also, a single trolley track went up the street. Miss Dodge inherited the property from her two aunts, Miss Charlotte Morgan and Miss Sarepth Morgan. When she passed on, she left her residence at 265 Franklin Street as a home for aged women. The home opened in December 1933, and since has been discontinued. This is a fine example of Victorian architecture. (Marie Wood.)

IS THIS BOSTON'S "BIG DIG?" No, it is the encasing of the Ell Pond Brook in back of Main Street stores including the Eastern Bank, from East Foster Street to Grove Street. The brook continues to the Malden River, Malden. The area is now the Grove Street parking lot.

AN EARLY CANNON. This cannon is located on Crystal Street, at the former veterans' building. (Marie Wood.)

DAMAGED BY FIRE, AUGUST 1968. The Warren Homestead at the corner of Essex and Myrtle Streets was dismantled by the owner. The home was built before 1900 and was occupied by the late Dr. Julius Clark, and later by his daughter, the late Mrs. Anita Warren. It is shown here while being demolished. Today it is the site of Shaw's Supermarket parking lot.

A VIEW OF ELL POND IN THE EARLY 1900s. In the early days of the town the pond contained very pure water and was bordered by ice houses. In the 1800s, ice from Melrose was sent to the tropics via clipper ships.

34

Four
SCHOOLS, ETC.

WHAT'S THE MATTER WITH THE MACHINE?

THE HORACE MANN SCHOOL, 40 DAMON AVENUE. Children run excitedly at the end of another school day.

THE COOLIDGE SCHOOL, MAIN STREET. The school opened in September 1979 for the last time, and the building is now filled with apartments.

A Committee of Students Welcome Eighth Graders on Opening Day at the Melrose Voke School.

A View of the Former High School when It became Melrose Middle School.

A Photo of the Scholarship Committee Headed by Mayor James Milano.

Schoolchildren with Melrose Superintendent of Schools David Driscoll. The children were working on a photography project.

A View of Newhall Shoes, a Melrose Landmark. Pottle Flower Shop is now on the site, 543–547 Main Street in the downtown Melrose Historical District.

Fells Hall. In the 1880s, Elisha Converse built Fells Hall for the convenience of his hundreds of employees, on the corner of Goodyear Avenue (Banks Place) and Main Street. The Ensign Thomas Lynde House was directly across Goodyear Avenue. It became a meeting hall, and church services were held there. It was a post office for a while, and classes were held there until Converse School was built. This photo was taken in the 1900s. A general store selling gasoline for 14¢ was directly across from the Pine Banks Tourists Camp.

A Photo of Melrose's Wyoming Station. From the book *Ancient Melrose*, the first train over the Boston & Maine Railroad Extension left Boston for Malden (Melrose) on July 4, 1845. It was a one-track road with wood-burning locomotives that had to "wood and water" almost every 10 miles. Wyoming had no station until the citizens built one by subscription. It was called "Boardman's Crossing" and if you wished to board a train there, you had to stand on the track and wave a white handkerchief. The railcrossing attendant's shack can be seen in the distance.

"Cascades." Located on lower Washington Street, in the spring the Cascades becomes a miniature rapids, gushing down the slopes.

STUDENTS AT THE MELROSE FAITH EVANGELISTICAL CHURCH SCHOOL PRACTICING FOR A PLAY.

THE NEW OFFICES OF THE NEW ENGLAND TELEPHONE AND TELEGRAPH AT 56 WEST FOSTER STREET, MELROSE, MARCH 23, 1907. The New England Telephone Company occupied the building until 1948. When automatic dialing came into effect, the building became surplus. A large exchange was opened on Elm Street, Malden. The city of Melrose, needing a larger police station, moved from city hall to the NETC building on West Foster Street. Today the police department needs larger quarters. Some folks miss the old four-party line; they cannot listen in on their neighbors' calls.

41

FELTON PLACE. Located off of Upham Street, Felton Place was turned into a mini-lake after a severe rain storm in October 1962. The lads were undoubtedly having a great time.

THE MELROSE RECYCLING COMMITTEE. From left to right, John F. Murphy Jr., Mary Ann Ryan, and Gail Wagner are pictured with Mayor James Milano in April 1988.

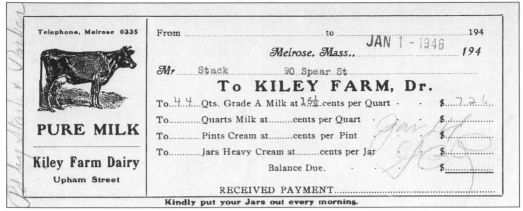

DAIRY RECEIPTS FROM THE KILEY FARM DAIRY ON UPHAM STREET. Grade-A milk was priced at 16.5¢ per quart.

A MILK RECEIPT FOR 60 QUARTS OF MILK AT 7¢ PER QUART. The receipt is for S.A. Chisam, milk, cream, or buttermilk, at 18 Eighth Street. (Courtesy of Priscilla and Herbert Gray.)

CORNELIUS CASEY. A veteran of the Civil War, Casey is pictured here surrounded by his friends.

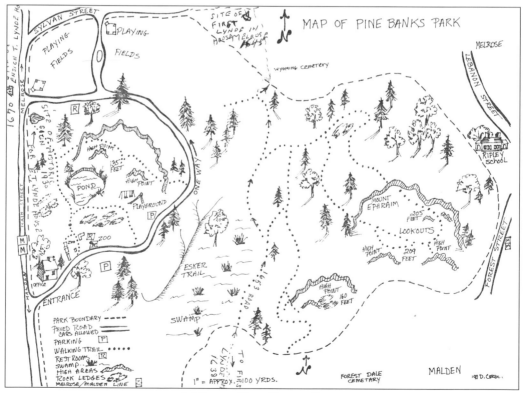

A MAP OF PINE BANKS PARK.

A View of Youle Street from the Corner of Otis and Vinton Streets, Taken in the Early Days of the Town. It is reported the fourth house from the left was the Stone Homestead at 31 Youle Street, and was the first house built in that section of Melrose. The old Larrabee Farm was sold by the heirs of Beomi Vinton in 1805. (Elinor Giles Laudin.)

A Wall Being Constructed at Ell Pond to Prevent Erosion, 1987.

THE 50TH ANNIVERSARY CELEBRATION. In 1950, Melrose celebrated its 50th anniversary as a city. The celebration included a gala parade featuring many organizations. Large crowds watched the line march on Main Street.

THE WEST WYOMING AVENUE STABLES AFTER THE FIRE, OUR LAST RIDING STABLES.

Five

FACES AND PLACES

AFTER THE DELUGE WHAT?

A TRANQUIL POND LOCATED IN THE OLDER SECTION OF WYOMING CEMETERY BY THE CEMETERY OFFICE. The pond has been filled in and the old office replaced by the new stone building near the Sylvan Street entrance.

MEMBERS OF THE FIRE DEPARTMENT RECEIVING A CHECK FOR PROGRAMS. Pictured from left to right are Captain Edwin Wood, Chief Francis B. O'Brien, Sal Marotta, and Robert Batchelder.

Do You Recognize This Area? The city garages were formerly located in the parking lot in back of the fire station and city hall.

Melrose Laundry at The Waverley Building. The first Waverley Block was erected in the 1850s. In 1856, members of the newly established Trinity Episcopal Church held services in Waverley Hall. In 1863, the Wyoming Lodge of Masons, chartered in 1857, who first met in Lyceum Hall on Main Street, moved to the Waverley Block, to "handsomely furnished rooms with costly and appropriate paraphernalia." Also in 1863 the Waverley Royal Arch Chapter of Masons, taking its name from the Waverley Block, was formed. In 1865, the Hugh de Payens Commandery was established there.

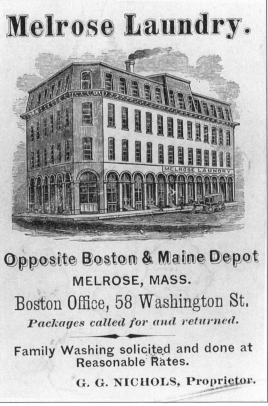

Melrose Laundry.

Opposite Boston & Maine Depot

MELROSE, MASS.

Boston Office, 58 Washington St.

Packages called for and returned.

Family Washing solicited and done at Reasonable Rates.

G. G. NICHOLS, Proprietor.

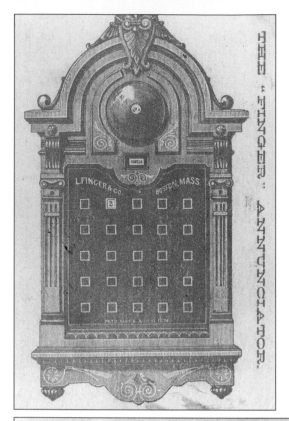

THE FINGER ANNUNCIATOR. Melrose made instruments for paging people.

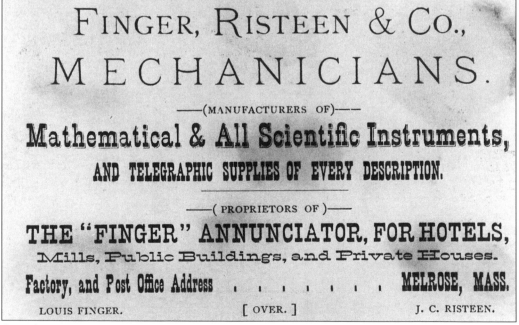

AN ADVERTISEMENT FOR FINGER, RISTEEN & CO., MECHANICIANS. The company manufactured mathematical and scientific instruments and telegraphic supplies of every description. The company owners were Louis Finger and J.C. Risteen.

A Photograph of Commander Robinson G.A.R., Deceased.

Collecting for a Cause. Members of the Mt. Hood Park Association collected toys for children's charities. Pictured from left to right are Derek McQuillan, Stephen Walsh (president), and Paul McQuillan.

A GIFT FROM THE CITIZENS. The urn located in front of city hall was presented to the city of Melrose in 1874 by Melrose citizens.

THE HOUSE AT 663 MAIN STREET. Located in the downtown Melrose Historic District, this building was constructed about 1881–83, and was used commercially. Longtime realtor W.W. MacIntosh operated out of the second floor, and the Melrose Red Cross occupied the first-floor offices.

THE ELL POND BROOK IN THE REAR OF THE WYOMING STATION, ON ITS WAY TO THE MALDEN RIVER. (Marie Wood.)

MELROSE SQUARE IN A VIEW FROM THE COCHRANE HOUSE, GROVE STREET, MELROSE. The building in the right foreground has been renovated.

YMCA LADIES IN GAY NINETIES ATTIRE PREPARING FOR THEIR AUCTION. These members are, from left to right, Ruth Hussey, Anne Lucas, Kathleen Gorman, Peg Trembley, and Janice Baldi.

THE MELROSE CIVIL DEFENSE UNIT MARCHING IN A PARADE. The unit was organized at the beginning of World War II.

RICHARD QUINLAN RECEIVING FLEA FESTIVAL PROCEEDS.

THE MELROSE PUBLIC LIBRARY READING ROOM, WEST EMERSON STREET. Built in 1904, the library was made possible from a grant given by Andrew Carnegie. The library is on the former site of the first Melrose High School, which burnt down in 1897.

THE MELROSE FLORIST COMPANY. Formerly located at 245 West Wyoming Avenue, the florist shop and green house were demolished and have been replaced by the Joseph T. Cefalo Memorial Complex.

A PROMOTION BEING GIVEN TO CHIEF FRANCIS B. O'BRIEN. Shown here are, left to right, Lt. Fred Ward, Ed Kenny, Capt. Gerard O'Neil, Harold Packard, Chief O'Brien, Al Garrant, Mayor Milano, John Bushee, and Capt. Edwin Wood. (Capt. John O'Brien.)

56

Six

PUBLIC SAFETY

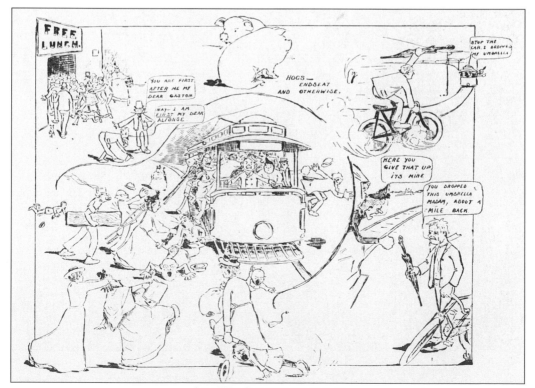

ARE WE COMING TO THIS?

THE MELROSE HIGH SCHOOL BAND IN A LOCAL PARADE.

A. WILBUR LYNDE, A MEMBER OF THE 42ND MASS.
VOLUNTEER INFANTRY, G.A.R.

A Sons of Italy Gathering, c. 1974. Pictured left to right are John Cinella, Bill Robinson, Louis Gibelli, Mayor James Milano, Michael Festa, and Frank Schuraffa.

The Prince Men Chorus of Melrose V.F.W. 1506, 428 Main Street. The men are singing aboard a large flat-bed truck in the Fourth of July parade. (Norman Prince Post.)

THE MELROSE HIGH SCHOOL BAND PLAYING AT THE 1990 GRADUATION.

THE MELROSE BEAUTY ACADEMY. On the site of present-day Papa Gino's, the Melrose Beauty Academy was located at 417 Main Street, Melrose.

A View of the Building at 22 Corey Street. The National Company occupied the building at this period. Over the years it has encountered many uses.

New Developments. The new department of public works garage was being constructed on Tremont Street when this photograph was taken in October 1978.

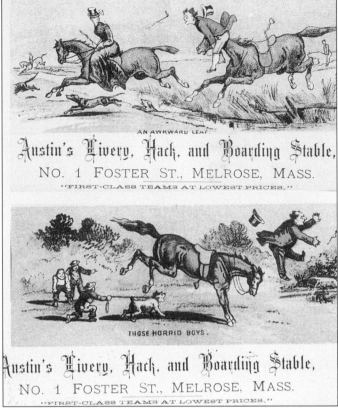

AN AWKWARD LEAP

Austin's Livery, Hack, and Boarding Stable,
NO. 1 FOSTER ST., MELROSE, MASS.
"FIRST-CLASS TEAMS AT LOWEST PRICES."

THOSE HORRID BOYS.

Austin's Livery, Hack, and Boarding Stable,
NO. 1 FOSTER ST., MELROSE, MASS.
"FIRST-CLASS TEAMS AT LOWEST PRICES."

SOUVENIR CARDS. These were given to customers by Austin's Livery, Hack, and Boarding Stable, No 1 Foster Street, Melrose. "First Class Teams At Lowest Prices." (P. & H. Gray.)

THE FIRST MAYOR, LEVI GOULD. Pictured here is Levi Gould, the first mayor of Melrose, when it became a city in 1900. Levi was very active in the Melrose Town era.

Seven
INTERESTING SCENES

NIGHT STREET LIGHTS.

AUTOMATIC RADIO. Shown here is an aerial view of the Automatic Radio building at 2 Main Street across from Pine Banks Park. Other companies have succeeded Automatic Radio. The zoo cages are at the bottom of this picture.

FORMER-GOVERNOR EDWARD KING VISITS MELROSE. Citizens present at the visit included former-mayor James Milano.

FORMER MELROSE CHAMBER OF COMMERCE PRESIDENT FELIX TESTA. Testa is pictured here addressing members.

PREPARING THE CONSTRUCTION SITE FOR THE MCCARTHY SENIOR CITIZEN APARTMENTS AT 910 MAIN STREET, MELROSE.

FRANK C. PIERCE SR., TUGBOAT CAPTAIN IN THE BOSTON NAVAL SHIPYARD. Pierce served one year as a mate aboard a Boston fire boat, and in 1917 became captain in the Boston Naval Shipyard with the tug *James Wooley*, under contract to the U.S. Navy. For many years Frank was the tugboat captain and pilot on the Navy tug *Nottaway*. He guided battleships and great liners in and out of Boston Harbor. Pierce moved his family to Melrose in 1923 and lived at 340 East Foster Street. The residence remained in his family until 1979.

THE U.S. NAVY TUG NOTTAWAY, FRANK C. PIERCE SR., CAPTAIN.

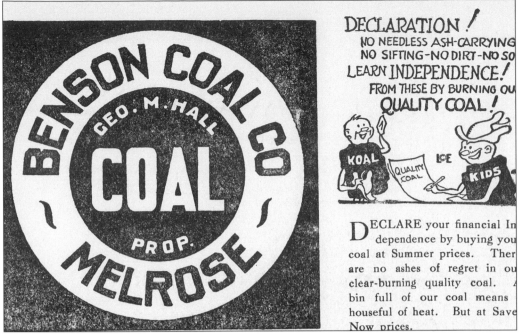

AN ADVERTISEMENT OF THE BENSON COAL COMPANY, 20 TREMONT STREET. The company's quality merchandise since 1870 has included coal, coke, and wood.

MELROSE WAKEFIELD HOSPITAL. In need of more space, the hospital constructed an additional wing for medical care.

ALVIN CHASE, A CIVIL WAR VETERAN OF THE 16TH REGIMENT, NEW HAMPSHIRE VOLUNTEERS. While on campaign in Louisiana, he contracted a severe illness and was sent home, where he died shortly thereafter. This photograph was taken of the deceased placed in a standing position, dressed in his uniform, and held up by hidden supports. Chase was the great-grandfather of Madeline Edmonds of Melrose. (Madeline Edmonds.)

A VIEW OF THE OCTAGON HOUSE. Located on East Wyoming Avenue, the house can be seen in the upper left-hand corner of this picture. It was the home of W.P. Sargent, and it was demolished c. 1900. In the foreground is Main Street.

MEMORIAL DAY SERVICES, MELROSE JUNIOR HIGH. Melrose Junior High Principal congratulates Master of Ceremonies Felix Sagarino on his 92nd birthday, May 23, 1986.

INSTALLING RAILROAD GATES AT WYOMING AVENUE. This marked the end of gatekeepers guarding the traffic for approaching trains.

THE MELROSE HIGH SCHOOL PLAYING FIELD AFTER A SEVERE RAIN STORM.

THE NEW CEMETERY OFFICE. Shown here is the new cemetery office in Melrose's Wyoming Cemetery.

Reservoir at Bear Hill, Metropolitan Park System, Malden, Mass.

THE RESERVOIR AT BEAR HILL, METROPOLITAN PARK SYSTEM, MALDEN. The water from this reservoir serves Malden and Melrose.

MEMORABILIA TABLE OF THE MELROSE CLASS OF 1929.

WHERE ARE WE? The sign announces foot traffic to the parking area between the buildings on Essex Street. The Powder Puff was demolished and the home in the back eliminated.

Eight
SPORTS, ETC.

"STOP THE FLOOD."

THE INTRODUCTION OF THE NEW MANAGER, MR. FLYNN, OF THE MELROSE MOUNT HOOD GOLF CLUB. Pictured from left to right are Mayor Milano, Mr. Flynn, Mr. Harry McCracken (president of the MGA), and Mr. Bill Ball (chairman of the Melrose Park Commission).

PIZZA MANIA. The great popularity of pizza in recent years has brought an influx of pizza stores in Melrose.

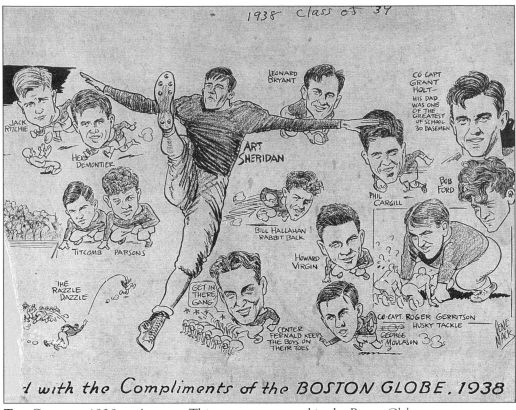

THE CLASS OF 1939 IN ACTION. This cartoon appeared in the *Boston Globe*.

FROM ANCIENT MELROSE. The new William Emerson House on the corner of Main and Emerson Streets was occupied by his family in November 1805. In this old inn, all of Emerson's children were born, except William and Isaac.

PAR FOR THE COURSE. A group of avid Melrose golfers receive instruction on how to improve their games.

LINCOLN SCHOOL STUDENTS. Students are seen enjoying a recess period on the school playground.

THE MELROSE BLUE KNIGHTS, A TEAM IN THE YOUTH HOCKEY CITY LEAGUE.

THE NEWLY COMPLETED M.D.C. SWIMMING POOL ON TREMONT STREET, MELROSE.

MOUNT HOOD. Children are seen here frolicking on snowy slopes at Mount Hood. The incarnation church spire is in the distance.

THE LIFE STATION. The station was equipped with a life-saving boat donated by the America Legion Auxiliary to the city on May 28, 1941, for use on Ell Pond. Mrs. Cora Trickey, who had witnessed a drowning a few years earlier, presented the keys to Mayor Robert A. Perkins. The event climaxed a year's worth of work by the community chairperson, Mrs. Madeline Knight. (Marie Wood.)

THE FIREFIGHTERS OF MELROSE. The men break the windows on the second floor of a Main Street building to vent smoke as flames pour out of the building.

DEMOLISHING THE OLD WYOMING RAILROAD WAITING ROOM STATION, 1983.

Special Attention paid to Children's Hair-Cutting.

WILLIAM T. KIRMES'

Hair-Cutting and Shaving Room,

CIGARS AND TOBACCO.

Waverley Building, Opp. Melrose Depot,

MELROSE.

AN ADVERTISING CARD FOR WILLIAM T. KIRMES, HAIR CUTTING AND SHAVING ROOM. The business was located in the Waverly Building opposite the Melrose Depot. (Priscilla and Herbert Gray.)

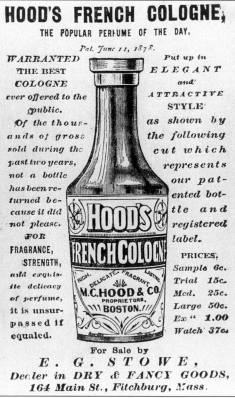

HOOD'S FRENCH COLOGNE. This cologne, a popular perfume of the day, was made in Melrose and patented June 11, 1878. The factory was located on the corner of Winthrop and Myrtle Streets. (Priscilla and Herbert Gray.)

THE MELROSE SENIOR COOKOUT. The cookout was held at the Knights of Columbus Hall before Milano Center was built.

A DISTINGUISHED GROUP. We were told this may be a photo of an Eastern Star Meeting. Are we correct?

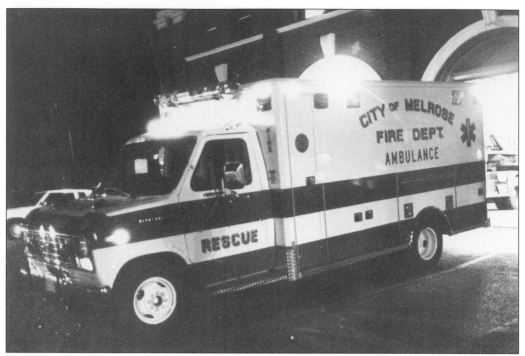

A FINE ADDITION. The new City of Melrose Fire Department ambulance arrived in December 1985.

THE MASSACHUSETTS COMM. MILITARY DIV. NATIONAL GUARD ARMY RECRUITING AND RETENTION BUILDING, 120 MAIN STREET, MELROSE.

GETTYSBURG BATTLE FIELD. The Lt. Col. Clark Baldwin Memorial is located on the battlefield at Gettysburg, Pennsylvania. Baldwin helped save the day for the Union on July 2, 1863. In gratitude, the monument was created. He was buried in Wyoming Cemetery, November 10, 1890. The Melrose gravestone is a smaller version of the Gettysburg monument. (Mildred Baldwin.)

THE REVERSE SIDE OF THE GETTYSBURG MONUMENT. Lt. Col. Clark Baldwin occupied this spot in support of a skirmish in the brigade line, and was engaged until the close of the action. Twenty seven soldiers died, 80 were wounded, and 15 taken prisoner. (Mildred Baldwin.)

MELROSE FRIENDS OF SCOUTING. These members gathered for a committee meeting.

THE BOARDMAN BUILDING. Workmen prepare to restore the Boardman Building, located at the corner of Main and Essex Streets. There was once a "Melrose Temperance Saloon" in the block.

MELROSE SQUARE. Shown here is Melrose Square looking toward Malden in 1987. The Massbank is on the left corner at West Foster Street; the Greenwood Building is on the right corner. The Victorian-style street lights add charm to the scene.

THE MELROSE COOPERATIVE BANK. The bank was chartered on April 4, 1890, and opened for business on April 20 of that same year. It was located at 160 Franklin Street until 1896, when it was moved to the Melrose Town Hall. In 1899, the bank moved to 543 Main Street, where it remained until 1937. After buying and remodeling the Chester S. Patten Building at 636–642 Main Street, the bank opened January 2, 1937.

THE MAIN STREET ARCO STATION. The Arco Station is no longer in business, and the site is now occupied by a Dunkin Doughnuts.

THE TRIMOUNT COMPANY. The company is blasting in a quarry in the spring of 1983. Mt. Hood Park is above the quarry.

THE CENTRAL FIRE STATION. A row of happy youngsters sitting on the side of the fire wagon are watching a demonstration.

THE FORMER SITE OF THE ENSIGN THOMAS LYNDE HOUSE AT 86 MAIN STREET. This is now the location of the Hunt Photo Company.

PINE BANKS. This postcard is from the Pine Banks Reservation, Melrose and Malden.

FLASHING LIGHTS, INSTALLED TO CAUTION VEHICLES APPROACHING LOCAL SCHOOLS.

DAMAGE FROM THE HURRICANE OF 1938. Many trees were felled in Melrose.

THE DEVASTATION OF THE HURRICANE. Trees near the library on West Emerson Street came down, and many people in southern New England were killed as a result of the 1938 hurricane.

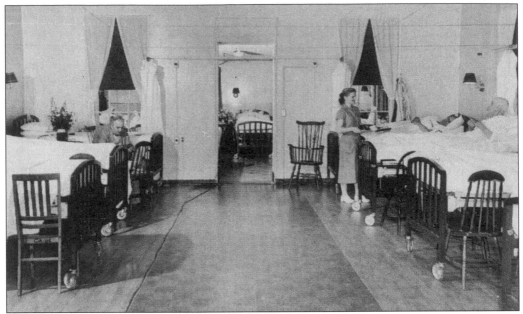

THE MEN'S WARD, MELROSE WAKEFIELD HOSPITAL. Shown here is a typical ward *c.* 1929.

A CAST MADE BY THE BOSTON SCULPTURE COMPANY, MELROSE. The company made many historical plaques, including a plastic cast of Washington crossing the Delaware.

THE BANDSTAND. Many concerts were performed at the bandstand, located on Ell Pond, Main Street.

CARUSO'S PIZZA SHOP. Don displays the art of making pizza while children anxiously await a slice.

WEST EMERSON STREET. This photo shows a view of the stores on West Emerson Street adjacent to the Waverly Building.

AN OLD BUILDING ON WASHINGTON STREET. J. Motkin & Sons occupied the premises at the time this photograph was taken.

THE 1939 MELROSE FOOTBALL TEAM, CLASS OF 1940. The team had many fine players, as seen in this drawing.

DO YOU RECOGNIZE ANYONE PICTURED HERE?

Massachusetts Committee On Public Safety
BOSTON, MASSACHUSETTS

OFFICIAL
IDENTITY CARD

PROPERTY OF MELROSE COMM.
ON PUBLIC SAFETY

Name ELFRIEDA ELOUISE SCARBOROUGH   Height 5' 6½"
Address 28 SYLVAN STREET   Weight 115
City MELROSE MASS.   Eyes HAZEL
Place of Birth BOSTON MASS.   Build SLIGHT
Date of Birth JULY 1, 1905   Comp. LIGHT   Number 5 B 2   2215
Nationality AMERICAN   Hair BLONDE
Office MELROSE 5 B 2
Division PROTECTION WOMEN A R WARDENS
Position DEPUTY WARDEN   Signature *Elfrieda Elouise Scarborough*

SERVING IN THE WAR. This is the official identity card of Elfrieda Scarborough, who was a deputy air raid warden during World War II.

THE MELROSE HIGHLAND TRAIN DEPOT OF YESTERYEAR. The Steele House is in the background; the station waiting room in the foreground has been removed. The train has been taken over by the T.

MAIN STREET, MELROSE SQUARE. The street is decorated with lights for the Christmas season.

THE MANSARD ROOF HOME AT 53 ELM STREET, BUILT C. 1852. Various owners occupied the house through the years. Notice the man posing on the antique tricycle or "velocipede." The owners of the house in 1893 were Mr. and Mrs. Wm. H. Waldron. (Karen Martino.)

THE MELROSE AMERICAN ALL-STAR TEAM, DISTRICT 12 BASEBALL CHAMPIONS. The team placed third in the the state tournament, with a record of 10 wins and 2 losses. Pictured from left to right are the following: (front row) Paul Lever, Joe Crowley, Joe Mercer, Ray Jones, Rich Green, Scott Drago, John Cinella, and bat boy Chris Cinella; (middle row) Keith Willworth, John DeCecca, Andy Gorton, Brian Grovo, Tom Boucher, Mark Pittella, Brian Bemis, and Steve Fogarty; (back row) Manager Eddie Weeks and Coach Vin Fogarty. Missing from the picture is Coach Phil Churchill. (Churchill American Little League.)

THE TRAFFIC LIGHT NEAR MAIN AND UPHAM STREETS. Notice the trolley tracks, which turned at Essex Street.

Concepts and Comments

A Reader for Students of English
as a Second Language

Second Edition

Patricia Ackert
Anne L. Nebel

THOMSON
™
HEINLE

Australia Canada Mexico Singapore Spain United Kingdom United States

VP/Publisher	Rolando Hernández-Arriessecq
Program Director	Susan Marshall
Editorial Coordinator	Jennifer Ryan
Developmental Editor	Kathleen Schultz
Project Editor	John Haakenson
Production Manager	Diane Gray
Art Director	Burl Sloan
Photo Researcher	Cheri Throop

Cover image based on photo by Masaaki Kazama

Photo Credits: Page 2, © Alan Levenson/Tony Stone Worldwide; 11, © Michael Newman/PhotoEdit; 20, © Superstock; 30, © Mark Green/Tony Stone Worldwide; 40, © 1994 C. Ron Chapple/FPG International, © 1993 Rob Gage/FPG International, © Lori Adamski Peek/Tony Stone Images; 41, The Bettmann Archive; 49, © 1940 Jack Breed/FPG International; 58, The Bettmann Archive; 68, © Gary Conner/PhotoEdit; 78, Nathaniel Dance (copy after) Portrait of Captain Cook, c. 1800 (original in National Maritime Museum, Greenwich, England) (DN 84800), National Library of Australia, Canberra, Australia; 88, © James Balog/Tony Stone Images; 98, © Tony Freeman/PhotoEdit; 99 © David Young-Wolff/PhotoEdit; 107, © Michael Newman/PhotoEdit; 117, © Paul Conklin/PhotoEdit; 128, © Tony Stone Images; 139, © Mark Richards/PhotoEdit, © Tony Freeman/PhotoEdit; 149, © Reuters/Bettmann; 159, © Michael Newman/PhotoEdit; 171, © UPI/Corbis/Bettmann; 182, © Anna E. Zuckerman/PhotoEdit; 190, © 1982 Tom Tracy/FPG International, © James Levin/FPG International; 201, © Andy Sacks/Tony Stone Images; 209, © Palmer/Kane/Tony Stone Images; 218, © Keystone View Company/FPG International; 228, © Jack Grove/PhotoEdit; 236, © Michael Rosenfeld/Tony Stone Images.

ISBN: 0-15-599718-1

Library of Congress Catalogue Number: 96-80057

Printed in the United States of America

2 3 4 5 6 039 10

Contents

To the Student

Concepts and Comments has 25 short readings and many kinds of activities. You will use this book to talk, read, and write about interesting topics. You will learn new words and improve your reading skills. We hope you enjoy this book.

Concepts and Comments, Second Edition is an engaging reading text for high-beginning to low-intermediate students of English as a foreign or second language. The text features 25 thematic units on a variety of topics, ranging from the culture specific to the universal.

Each unit presents a short reading and plentiful activities that focus on predicting, comprehension, finding main ideas, understanding details, and making inferences. The text introduces approximately 1,000 target vocabulary items—in both the readings and in the word study activities—and guides students in using context clues to discover meaning.

A main feature of this text is that the vocabulary items are systematically recycled throughout. Therefore, it is recommended that the units are studied in the sequence presented in the text, so students are not overwhelmed by new vocabulary items.

The text assumes an understanding of basic structures and vocabulary. All verb tenses except the future perfect are used. Personal pronouns, including the reflexive forms, past participles as adjectives, gerunds, and such connectors as *even though, however, yet,* and *so* are used.

A companion volume, **Insights and Ideas, Second Edition** is also available.

ACTIVITY TYPES

Pre-reading

Each unit begins with a series of pre-reading questions to generate interest and give students a reason for exploring the topic. The questions encourage students to share background knowledge and express opinions about the unit topic.

To further stimulate discussion and spark interest, each unit opens with a photograph, illustration, and/or map.

The Reading

Most of the unit readings are approximately five hundred words in length; however, in order to give students more extended reading experiences, a few readings are slightly longer. Although many of the readings are on familiar topics, they often present new or little-known information that will intrigue students.

Working with Vocabulary

This section in each unit includes the following two activity types:

Focus on the Reading. This activity identifies approximately twelve new words and asks students to practice using them in the context of the reading.

Focus on New Contexts. Students practice using the new words in different contexts. (Note that the words are used repeatedly throughout the other activities in the unit and in the units that follow.)

Understanding the Reading

This section in each unit includes the following three activity types:

Comprehension Questions. These ask for specific information from the reading. They help students review the main points of the reading, and allow the instructor to gauge the students' level of understanding. Some of the questions might require students to make inferences based on information presented in the reading. (All questions or activity items of this nature are preceded by an asterisk [*].) The questions can be answered orally or in writing and can easily be assigned for homework.

Details. Several formats, including true/false and multiple choice, are used to focus students' attention on specific details in the reading. This activity type gives students many opportunities to practice the essential reading skills of skimming and scanning for information.

Main Ideas. This activity type gives students practice in identifying the main ideas of the reading. This reading skill is often difficult for students, and it is helpful to discuss with them the difference between main ideas and supporting details. In a few units, the students must categorize information from the reading into main ideas and supporting details.

Writing

Each unit features an activity that integrates writing with the development of reading skills. These guided writing activities are clearly related to the unit topic and provide meaningful contexts for students to use new words and respond to the topic. The writing tasks are well-defined and range in variety from paragraphs, time lines, and lists to advertisements, journal entries, and postcards. The product of the writing activities provides another source of related reading material for the class.

WORD STUDY SECTIONS

The word study section in each unit is designed to enhance and reinforce students' understanding of English structures and word forms and to expand their vocabulary. Some of the activities deal with prefixes and suffixes and demonstrate how many English words can change in form. All of the words presented in these activities are based on new words from the readings. Other activities provide practice with prepositions, irregular verb forms, and identifying antecedents of noun substitutes.

A helpful index to the work study activities is provided on page 248.

BUILDING VOCABULARY SKILLS

The final section of each unit includes the following two activity types:

Vocabulary Review. This activity type is a quick review of new words from previous units. The format includes matching synonyms or antonyms, sentence completions, and multiple choice.

Context Clues. The ability to figure out the meaning of words from context is a key skill, and as students become more proficient at it, they become more efficient readers. This activity type provides additional practice in using context clues. The words that students encounter here are actually new vocabulary items that appear in the succeeding unit. The goal of this exercise is for students to develop their ability to guess the meaning of words from context while they read. Make sure that students understand that they should not use a dictionary for this activity.

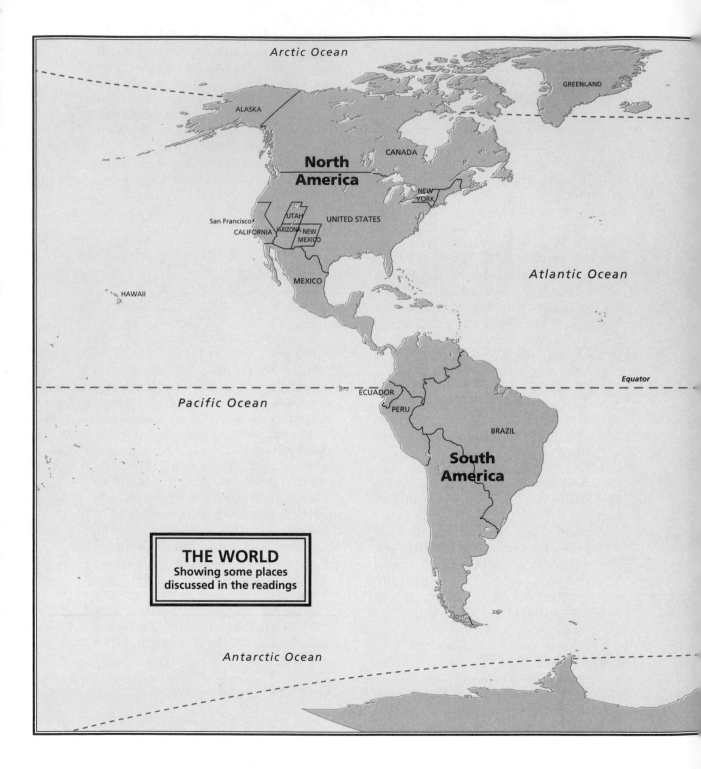

Arctic Ocean

GREENLAND

ALASKA

CANADA

North America

NEW YORK

San Francisco

UTAH

CALIFORNIA

ARIZONA

NEW MEXICO

UNITED STATES

Atlantic Ocean

HAWAII

MEXICO

ECUADOR

PERU

Equator

Pacific Ocean

BRAZIL

South America

THE WORLD
Showing some places
discussed in the readings

Antarctic Ocean

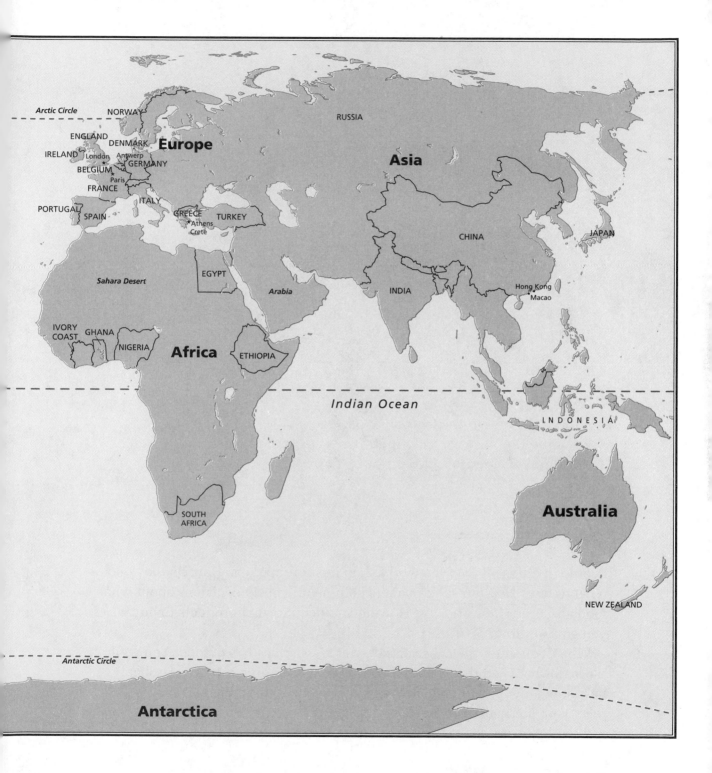

Arctic Circle

NORWAY

ENGLAND

DENMARK

IRELAND London Antwerp

Europe

GERMANY

BELGIUM

Paris

FRANCE

PORTUGAL

ITALY

SPAIN

GREECE

TURKEY

Athens

Crete

RUSSIA

Asia

CHINA

JAPAN

Sahara Desert

EGYPT

Arabia

INDIA

Hong Kong

Macao

IVORY
COAST

GHANA

NIGERIA

Africa

ETHIOPIA

Indian Ocean

INDONESIA

Australia

SOUTH
AFRICA

NEW ZEALAND

Antarctic Circle

Antarctica

Unit 1

Supermarket Marketing

Pre-reading

1. Where do you go to buy food and groceries?
2. Describe the markets and supermarkets in your country.
3. How do you choose which products to buy?

People in cities all over the world shop in supermarkets. How do they decide what to buy? How do supermarkets help people make decisions about what food and other items to buy? How do you decide what products to buy when you go shopping?

5   When you enter the supermarket, you see shelves full of food. You walk in the aisles between the shelves, pushing your shopping cart. You probably hear soft, slow music in the supermarket. This kind of music is playing to relax you and make you walk slowly. If you hear fast music, you will probably walk quickly and leave the supermarket after a short time. Supermarket

10   managers know that if they play slow, relaxing music in the store, people will probably stay longer and buy more food.

Where do you go in the supermarket when you first arrive? Many people go to the meat section first. This area of the store has many different kinds of meat. Some kinds are expensive and others are not. Usually, some kind of
15   meat is on sale—it has a special low price. The manager of the store knows where customers usually enter the meat section. The meat on sale is usually at the other end of the section, away from where the customers enter. If you want to buy this specially priced meat, you have to walk by the more expensive meat first. Maybe you will see something that you want to buy
20   before you reach the cheaper, inexpensive meat. Then you will spend more money in the meat section.

The dairy section sells milk and milk products such as butter and cheese. Many customers like milk that is low in fat. Some supermarkets sell three different containers of low-fat milk. Each container looks different, but each
25   contains the same product. One says "1% fat," one says "99% fat free," and one says "low-fat" in big letters and "1%" in very small letters. If you look carefully you can see that all the milk has the same amount of fat, and each container is the same size. The prices of all three should be the same. However, in many stores these three containers of milk would each have a
30   different price. The store will make more money if a customer chooses the milk that costs the most.

Most of the food in supermarkets is very attractive. People stop to look at products in attractive containers. If they don't look carefully at the prices and the contents of each container, they might spend more money. The next time
35   you are in the supermarket, pay attention to how the products are arranged on the shelves and in the different sections. Read the packages and containers. Remember, many products will say, "Buy me!" Stop and think. Which ones are the best value for your money?

WORKING WITH VOCABULARY

A. Focus on the Reading

Choose the best word or phrase for each sentence. If you need help, look at the reading again. (Use each word or phrase only once.)

aisles	containers	decide	products
amount	customers	however	section
attractive	dairy	on sale	shelves

1. People in cities all over the world shop in supermarkets. How do they _____*decide*_____ what to buy?

2. When you enter the supermarket, you see _____*shelves*_____ full of food.

3. You walk in the _____*aisles*_____ between the shelves, pushing your shopping cart.

4. Where do you go in the supermarket when you first arrive? Many people go to the meat _____*section*_____ first.

5. The meat that is on sale is usually at the other end of the department, away from where the _____*customers*_____ enter.

6. The _____*dairy*_____ department sells milk and milk products such as butter and cheese.

7. Some supermarkets sell three different _____*containers*_____ of low-fat milk.

8. The prices of all three should be the same. _____*However*_____, in many stores the three containers of milk each have a different price.

9. Most of the food in supermarkets is very _____*attractive*_____. People stop to look at it.

10. Remember, many _____*products*_____ will say, "Buy me!" Stop and think. Which ones are the best value for your money?

B. Focus on New Contexts

Here is more practice with the new words from the reading. Choose the best word or phrase for each sentence. (Use each word or phrase only once.)

aisle	containers	decide	section
amount	customers	on sale	shelves ✔
attractive	dairy	products	shopping cart

1. In a library there are thousands of books on the ___shelves___.
2. If you want to buy some children's books, you should go to the children's ___section___ of the bookstore.
3. Cheese, milk, and butter are three kinds of ___dairy___ products.
4. Clara bought a beautiful new dress. It was ___attractive___ for half price.
5. The supermarket is always busy on Saturdays. Most ___customers___ prefer to shop on the weekend.
6. Maria dropped a bottle of orange juice in the store yesterday. The bottle broke, and orange juice spread across the ___aisle___!
7. I can't ___decide___ what to have for lunch today. Do you want sandwiches or a salad?
8. Boxes, bottles, and cartons are three kinds of ___containers___.

UNDERSTANDING THE READING

A. Comprehension Questions

Answer the questions about the reading. If you need to, look at the article again.

1. How do you carry food when you shop in the supermarket?
2. What is on all of the shelves?
3. Who walks in the aisles and shops for food in a store?
4. What happens when you hear soft, slow music?

5. What does "on sale" mean?

6. Why are many food containers attractive?

B. Details

Circle the letter of the best answer.

Before you begin, look at items 5 and 6. They have asterisks (*) in front of them. The asterisk tells you that you cannot find the exact answer in the reading. To answer the question, you have to use information from the article *and* information you already know. You can find items like these throughout this book.

1. In the supermarket, people walk in the
   - a. shelves.
   - (c.) aisles.
   - b. dairy.
   - d. amount.

2. The manager knows
   - a. which customers like slow music.
   - b. which customers like low-fat milk.
   - c. how you decide which products to buy.
   - (d.) where customers enter the meat section.

3. When you walk by the expensive meat
   - (a.) maybe you will buy some.
   - c. you will buy dairy products.
   - b. you will not look at it.
   - d. maybe it is on sale.

4. The three different containers of low-fat milk
   - a. contain three different kinds of milk.
   - b. are all the same price.
   - c. are all on sale.
   - (d.) each have the same amount of fat.

*5. Supermarket managers make the food attractive so
   - a. it is cheap.
   - c. it is in the meat section.
   - b. it is in the dairy section.
   - (d.) the customers will buy more.

*6. Yogurt and chocolate milk are in the
   - a. meat section.
   - c. frozen-food section.
   - (b.) dairy section.
   - d. fruit-and-vegetable section.

C. Main Idea

Check (✔) the main idea of the reading. This is the most important idea of the reading.

_____ 1. Butter is in the dairy section.

__✓__ 2. The supermarket is designed to make you buy some things.

_____ 3. Customers push shopping carts in the aisles.

_____ 4. Most food in the supermarket is attractive.

WRITING

Here is a list of the sections in a supermarket. Can you guess what products you will find in each one? Work with a partner. Make a list of the kinds of food you would find in each supermarket section.

dairy section   frozen-food section
meat section   seafood section
produce section   bakery

WORD STUDY

A. Plural Nouns

When a noun ends in **f,** change the **f** to **v** and add **-es** to make it plural.

Here are two examples:

shelf   shelves   leaf   leaves

When a noun ends in **fe,** change the **fe** to **ve** and add **-s** to make it plural.

Here are two examples:

knife   knives   wife   wives

Exception: Do not change the word **roof.** Add **-s** only to make **roofs.**
Change the following nouns to make them plural.

1. loaf _loaves_
2. shelf _shelves_
3. wife _wives_

4. life _lives_
5. roof _roofs_
6. knife _knives_

B. Prepositions

The preposition **to** shows movement toward something.

Here are some examples:

Many customers go **to** the meat section first.

Sylvia goes **to** the movies once a week.

The preposition **in** shows a place or location. It can also mean "inside
something."

Here are some examples:

Milk is **in** the dairy section.

My homework is **in** my notebook.

Complete each sentence with the preposition **to** or **in.**

1. People in cities all over the world shop _in_ supermarkets.
2. Cheese is _in_ the dairy section.
3. The manager goes _to_ the supermarket every day.
4. Customers usually stay _in_ the supermarket for about an hour.
5. John was born _in_ 1970.
6. Our English classes end _in_ June.
7. I often walk _to_ class.
8. It is very warm _in_ our classroom today.
9. Do you live _in_ an apartment or a house?
10. Mimi never comes _to_ school early.

C. Word Forms

In English, every sentence must have a subject and a verb. The subject of a sentence is usually a noun or pronoun. Sometimes nouns and verbs have similar forms. Sometimes they have the same form. Look at the lists of nouns and verbs.

SIMILAR FORMS		SAME FORMS	
Verb	**Noun**	**Verb**	**Noun**
manage	manager	cost	cost
drive	driver	drink	drink
re teach	teacher	work	work
re work	worker	circle	circle
own	owner	*re* cook	cook

Notice that all of the nouns under "Similar Forms" end in **-er** and name people.

Now complete each sentence with the correct noun form.

manage   1. A supermarket ___*manager*___ works very hard.

work   2. I will call you after I finish my ___work___ at home.

work   3. A factory ___worker___ works very long hours.

teach   4. We have a new ___teacher___ at our school this year.

drink   5. Let's go to the cafeteria. I want to buy a ___drink___. I'm thirsty.

cost   6. That meat is on sale. The ___cost___ is very low.

cook   7. The ___cook___ at the new Chinese restaurant is from Hong Kong.

own   8. The new ___owner___ of the store near my house is very nice.

drive   9. A school bus _____ driver _____ must be very careful.

circle   10. If the directions say "Circle your answer," then you must draw a _____ circle _____ around the best answer.

BUILDING VOCABULARY SKILLS

Context Clues

You can often understand the meaning of a new word from the other words and information in the sentence or from nearby sentences. The other words that help you understand new words are called **context clues.**

For example, in paragraph 1 on page 3, you can find the meaning of the word **inexpensive.** What does **inexpensive** mean? When is meat in the supermarket **inexpensive?**

Practice using context clues. Tell the meaning of each word in **bold** (dark) print. These words are from Unit 2. (Do not use your dictionary.)

1. Danish and Norwegian are **similar** languages. If you speak one, you can understand the other. Chinese and English are not similar languages.

2. Our English class **lasts** for one hour. It starts at 9:00 and ends at 10:00.

3. I want to study at an American university. This is my **major** reason for studying English.

4. When you remember something, you keep it in your **mind.**

5. Before you do the laundry, you must **divide** the clothes into different groups of colors.

Unit 2

Memory

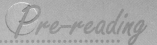

Pre-reading

1. What is your oldest memory?
2. What did you eat for dinner last Tuesday?
3. What things do you always remember? What things do you always forget?
4. What is memory?

"Memorize these words." "Learn this spelling rule." "Don't forget about the quiz tomorrow." You remember things every day, but how do you do it?

When you want to call a store or an office that you don't call often, you look in the telephone book for the number. You dial the number, and then you
5   forget it! You use your short-term memory to remember the number. Your short-term memory lasts about 30 seconds, or half a minute. However, you don't need to look in the telephone book for your best friend's number

because you already know it. This information is in your long-term memory.
Your long-term memory has everything that you remember through the years.

10 Why do you forget things sometimes? Is there a reason? Yes, there are
several. The major reason for forgetting something is because you did not
learn it well in the beginning. For example, you meet some new people, and
right away you forget their names. You hear the names but you do not learn
them, so you forget them.

15 You can help yourself remember better. Here are some ideas.

1. Move information from your short-term memory to your long-term
   memory. You can do this if you practice the new information. Say it to
   yourself out loud. Think about it.

2. After you learn something, study it again and again. Learn it more than you
   need to. This process is called *overlearning.* For example, when you learn
   new words, practice using them in sentences. Don't try to memorize words
   from a list only.

3. Make sure that you understand new information. It is very difficult to
   remember something that you don't understand. Ask questions when you
   learn something new to be certain that you understand.

4. Do not listen to music or watch television when you study. You will
   remember better if you concentrate on one thing at a time.

5. Try to connect new information with something that you already know. For
   example, when you learn the name of a new kind of food, think of a similar
   kind of food that you already know.

6. Divide new information into several parts (about five or six). Learn one part
   at at time and stop for a few minutes. Don't sit down and try to learn a very
   large amount of new information all at once.

7. Try to make a picture in your mind. For example, if you hear or see a new
   word, make a picture of how it looks to you in your mind. This "mental"
   picture will help you remember that word the next time you see or hear it.

8. Think of word clues to help you remember information. One very helpful
   kind of word clue is an *acronym.* An acronym is a word formed from the

first letter of a group of words. For example, many American schoolchildren learn the names of the Great Lakes in North America by remembering the word *homes. Homes* is an acronym that comes from the names of the Great Lakes: <u>H</u>uron, <u>O</u>ntario, <u>M</u>ichigan, <u>E</u>rie, <u>S</u>uperior.

9. Relax when you study! Try to enjoy yourself. You are learning new things every minute. You will remember better if you are happy and relaxed.

WORKING WITH VOCABULARY

A. Focus on the Reading

Choose the best word for each sentence. If you need help, look at the reading again. (Use each word only once.)

acronym	divide	major	seconds
connect	lasts	mind	short-term
dial ✔	list	relax	similar

1. When you want to call a store or an office that you don't call often, you look in the telephone book for the number. You _____*dial*_____ the number, and then you forget it!

2. You use your short-term memory to remember the number. It _____lasts_____ about 30 seconds, or half a minute.

3. The _____major_____ reason for forgetting something is because you did not learn it well in the beginning.

4. When you learn new words, practice using them in sentences. Don't try to memorize words from a _____list_____ only.

5. Try to _____connect_____ new information with something that you already know.

6. For example, when you learn the name of a new kind of food, think of a kind of _____similar_____ food that you already know.

7. _____Divide_____ new information into several parts (about five or six). Learn one part at a time and stop for a few minutes.

8. Try to make a picture in your __mind__. For example, if you hear or see a new word, make a picture of how it looks to you.

9. An __acronym__ is a word formed from the first letter of a group of words.

10. __Relax__ when you study! Try to enjoy yourself. You will remember everything better.

B. Focus on New Contexts

Here is more practice with the new words from the reading. Choose the best word for each sentence. (Use each word only once.)

connect	divide	list	relax
describe	furniture	major	seconds
dial	lasts	mind	similar ✔

1. Lemons and limes are __similar__ fruits. They are the same shape and size. The only difference is that one is yellow and the other is green.

2. Edward usually reads in bed for an hour each night. Reading helps him __relax__ and fall asleep.

3. Before Kirsten goes shopping at the supermarket she always makes a __list__ of the food she wants to buy.

4. Sometimes when we are waiting for something time goes very slowly. The __seconds__ feel like minutes, and the minutes feel like hours!

5. Because Julia is very busy, she has to __divide__ her time carefully: She goes to school in the morning, works in the afternoon, and studies every evening.

6. I remember my last vacation so well! I can still see a picture of the beach in my __mind__.

7. I have never been to the mountains. I think they must be very beautiful.

   Can you _describe_ them to me? What do they look like?

UNDERSTANDING THE READING

A. Comprehension Questions

Answer the questions about the reading. If you need to, look at the article again.

1. Why do we forget new phone numbers?
2. Why do we remember our friends' phone numbers?
3. What is the major reason people forget things?
4. What is one way to help you remember better?
5. What is an acronym?

B. Details

Write **T** if the sentence is true and **F** if the sentence is false.

_F_   1. Short-term memory lasts about two minutes.   30 seconds

_T_ *2. Your address is in your long-term memory.

_F_   3. It is easy to memorize things that you don't understand.

_T_   4. You should study new words in sentences, not just in lists.

_T_   5. It is possible to move information from your short-term memory to your long-term memory.

C. Main Idea

Check (✔) the two main ideas of the reading. These are the most important ideas of the reading.

_____   1. It is easy to remember a telephone number.

__✓__   2. People have short-term and long-term memories.

__✓__   3. You can learn to remember better.

_____   4. It is important to remember people's names.

WRITING

What is your favorite memory? Is it a memory of a special place or person? Close your eyes and try to make a picture in your mind. Then write a few sentences to describe what you see. When you finish, exchange papers with another student and read about his or her favorite memory!

WORD STUDY

A. Negative Prefixes

The prefixes **un-, im-, in-, dis-,** and **non-** can be added to the beginning of some words. The prefixes mean "not."

Choose the correct word to complete each sentence.

disagree	inexpensive	unable	uninteresting
impossible	nonsmoker	uncomfortable	unsafe ✔
incomplete	nonstop	unhappy	untrue

1. The brakes on my car do not work. It is _____ *unsafe* _____ to drive.

2. Anne was _____ *unable* _____ to remember all her friends' birthdays. Finally, she bought a datebook and wrote down important information.

3. The advertisement in the paper for a sales clerk is _____ *incomplete* _____. It describes the job but doesn't give a telephone number.

4. This plane flies directly from London to New York without stopping. It is a _____ *nonstop* _____ flight.

5. My answer is different from yours. I _____ *disagree* _____ with you, but perhaps I am wrong.

6. I didn't like the movie last night. I almost fell asleep. It was very _____ *uninteresting* _____.

7. The chair I have at work is terribly _____ *uncomfortable* _____. If I sit in it for more than an hour my back begins to hurt.

8. The vegetarian restaurant on the corner is very ___inexpensive___.
   Two people can eat a nice dinner for very little money. And the food is
   great, too.

B. Prepositions

The preposition **at** shows location, or place.

Here is an example:

   Rita usually has dinner **at** home.

The preposition **at** is also used with time.

Here is an example:

   She has dinner **at** six o'clock every night.

   Note: **at** four-thirty   But: **in** the morning

         at noon   **in** the afternoon

         at midnight   **in** the evening

         at night

Complete each sentence with in, at, or to.

1. People all over the world shop ___in___ supermarkets.

2. In some cities, supermarkets are open 24 hours a day. Customers can
   shop ___in___ the morning, ___in___ the
   afternoon, or ___in___ the evening.

3. Please call me tonight ___at___ 8:00. My number is
   ___in___ the telephone book.

4. Bill usually studies ___at___ home, but sometimes he
   goes ___to___ the library.

5. I like to study ___in___ a quiet place, too. It helps me
   remember better.

6. You can learn to move information from your short-term memory
   ___to___ your long-term memory.

7. When you learn a new word, try to make a picture ___*in*___ your mind.

BUILDING VOCABULARY SKILLS

A. Vocabulary Review

Match the words in column A with their meaning in column B.

A		B
_c_	1. aisles	a. people who shop in a store
_d_	2. on sale	b. nice to look at
_e_	3. dairy products	c. the space where customers walk between the shelves
_a_	4. customers	
_b_	5. attractive	d. inexpensive
		e. milk, cheese, and butter

B. Context Clues

You can often understand the meaning of a new word from the other words and information in the sentence or from nearby sentences. The other words that help you understand the new words are called **context clues.**

Practice using context clues. Choose the answer that is closest in meaning to each word in **bold** print. These words are from Unit 3. (Do not use your dictionary.)

1. The Sahara Desert is a **huge** desert in Africa. It covers millions of square kilometers.
   a. new
   b. small
   c. very large
   d. very beautiful

2. The Andes Mountains **stretch** from Colombia to Chile.
   a. walk
   b. reach
   c. move
   d. grow

3. About 10,000 people live in the **town** of Watertown.
   a. street
   b. state
   c. country
   d. small city

4. The **United** States of America is a country of fifty states.

   a. different   c. divided

   (b.) joined together   d. country

5. When you take ice out of the freezer, it **melts.**

   a. changes to air   c. becomes colder

   (b.) changes to water   d. remains frozen

6. In the **century** from 1800 to 1900 people did not have cars or airplanes.

   a. ten years   c. a kind of money

   (b.) one hundred years   d. an old kind of car

7. Kimonos are **traditional clothes** from Japan. Today most Japanese wear modern clothes. They wear kimonos for special holidays.

   a. modern clothes

   (b.) old clothes

   c. special clothes for very cold weather

   d. special clothes that people in one culture have worn throughout history

Unit 3

Greenland

Pre-reading

1. Where is Greenland?
2. What do you think the weather is like there?
3. What is the midnight Sun?
4. What do you think life is like for the people in Greenland?

Greenland is the largest island in the world. It covers more than two million square kilometers. Imagine that a map of Greenland is on top of a map of Europe and Africa. Greenland would stretch from London to the middle of the Sahara Desert. Most of the island lies in the Arctic Circle, and a huge
5   sheet of ice covers 85 percent of it.

    The ice sheet is more than 1,500 meters thick, and it never melts. Probably only rock lies under this ice, but no one knows for sure. Along the coast, mountains rise from the sea. Huge pieces of ice, called glaciers, float in the

sea between the mountains. Some of them are as tall as ten-story buildings.
10   Because Greenland is so cold, it is not very green. There are a few low trees in
the southwest, but no real forests. In the winter, snow covers everything. In
the summer, very low plants cover the ground between the sea and the ice
sheet.

The first people to live in Greenland were probably Eskimos who came
15   from Canada about 3,000 years ago. Norwegian Vikings were the first
Europeans to see the island. They came in 875, but they did not build towns
and live there until 982. At the same time, another group of Eskimos came to
Greenland from Alaska. In 1261, the people in Greenland decided to join the
country of Norway. Then, in 1380, Norway united with Denmark. This union
20   ended in 1814, and Greenland stayed with Denmark. Today this huge island is
part of the kingdom of Denmark. Greenland is about fifty times as large as
Denmark, but Denmark has about ninety times as many people.

About 62,000 people live in Greenland. Most of them are part Eskimo and
part Danish. They call themselves Greenlanders and speak Greenlandic
25   language (which has many Danish words). Almost all of them live in towns
and villages along the southwestern coast because that is the warmest part of
the island. Life in Greenland is difficult because the weather is very cold.
Temperatures average −29.5 degrees Celsius (−29.5° C) in January, −10
degrees Celsius (−10° C) in July. It is dark 24 hours a day in the winter, but in
30   the summer the Sun shines all day and night. This is the time of the midnight
Sun.

The island has very few natural resources. The people raise a few kinds of
vegetables and sheep. The most important industry is fishing. In southwest
Greenland there are many fish stations and processing plants where fish are
35   cleaned, dried, salted, or frozen. Much of the processed fish is exported to
other countries.

Life in Greenland is changing fast. For centuries, people there had no
communication with the rest of the world. They had very traditional lives.
Today Greenland is much more modern. Many changes are taking place, and
40   some of them are difficult for the Greenlanders. It is not easy to move from a
traditional life to a modern life.

Today Greenland is important to the world because scientists study the
weather there. They can tell when storms are developing over the North
Atlantic Ocean. This weather information is important because the North

45 Atlantic is a busy shipping area. Greenland welcomes scientists from many countries of the world. Together these scientists are making important discoveries about how the weather on our planet is changing. Because of the work that scientists do in Greenland, people all over the world are learning more about the weather and the environment.

WORKING WITH VOCABULARY

A. Focus on the Reading

Choose the best word for each sentence. If you need help, look at the reading again. (Use each word only once.)

centuries	huge ✓	sheet ✔	traditional
communication	imagine	storms	union
degrees	melts	stretches	united
developing	resources	towns	weather

1. Most of Greenland lies in the Arctic Circle, and a huge _____*sheet*_____ of ice covers 85 percent of it.

2. Greenland is also very big. _____imagine_____ that a map of Greenland is on top of a map of Europe and Africa. Greenland _____stretches_____ from London to the middle of the Sahara.

3. The ice sheet is more than 1,500 meters thick, and it never _____melts_____.

4. _____Huge_____ pieces of ice, called glaciers, float in the sea between the mountains.

5. In 1261, the people of Greenland decided to join the country of Norway. Then, in 1380, Norway _____united_____ with Denmark. This _____union_____ ended in 1814.

6. About 62,000 people live in Geenland. Almost all of them live in _____towns_____ and villages along the southwestern coast because that is the warmest part of the island.

7. The island has very few natural ___resources___. People raise a few
   kinds of vegetables and sheep.

8. Life in Greenland is changing fast. For ___centuries___, people
   there had no ___communication___ with the rest of the world.

9. It is not easy to move from a ___tradicional___ life to a modern life.

10. Now Greenland is important to the world because scientists study the
    weather there. They can tell when storms are ___developing___ over
    the North Atlantic Ocean.

B. Focus on New Contexts

Here is more practice with the new words from the reading. Choose the best word
for each sentence. (Use each word only once.)

centuries	huge	sheet	traditional
communication ✔	imagine	southwest	union
degrees	melts ✔	stretches	united
developing	resources	towns	weather

1. Talking on the telephone and writing letters are two forms of
   ___communication___.

2. In Mexico, many beautiful little ___towns___ stretch along the
   Atlantic Coast. Tourists enjoy visiting them since they are much quieter
   than the big cities.

3. Last summer I went to Hawaii. Have you ever been to the
   ___United___ States?

4. ___Imagine___ that you live in Greenland. What would you do in
   the winter?

5. Forests, rivers, and petroleum are natural ___resources___.

6. Be careful if you drive in the winter! When the Sun shines and the
   snow ___melts___, a ___sheet___ of ice may develop
   on the road.

7. Texas and New Mexico are two states in the ___southwest___ United States.

UNDERSTANDING THE READING

A. Comprehension Questions

Answer the questions about the reading. If you need to, look at the article again.

*1. Where is Greenland?

2. What covers 85 percent of the island?

3. What are glaciers?

4. Who were the first people to live in Greenland?

5. What Kingdom is Greenland part of?

6. Why do most people live in the southwestern part of the island?

7. What is the weather like in Greenland?

8. Does the island have any natural resources?

9. What do scientists study in Greenland?

*10. How is life changing in Greenland?

B. Details

Circle the letter of the best answer.

1. Most of Greenland lies in
   a. Denmark.
   b. Europe.
   c. the Arctic Circle.
   d. the Sahara Desert.

2. The ice sheet
   a. melts in the summer.
   b. is always there.
   c. is three kilometers thick.
   d. has a few green plants under it.

3. Greenland
   a. is flat.
   b. has warm winters.
   c. is rich in natural resources.
   d. has mountains near the sea.

4. The first people to live in Greenland were

   a. Danes.   c. Norwegians.

   (b.) Eskimos.   d. scientists.

5. Greenland is important to the world because

   a. a huge sheet of ice covers it.

   b. it is part of Denmark.

   c. it has many trees and natural resources.

   (d.) scientists study the weather there.

6. Most people in Greenland are

   (a.) Eskimos.   c. Canadian and Danish.

   b. Vikings.   d. Danish and Eskimo.

C. Main Idea

Check (✔) the two main ideas of the reading. These are the most important ideas of the reading.

_____ 1. Greenland has a cold climate and few natural resources.

_____ 2. The ice sheet is 1,500 meters thick.

_____ 3. Life in Greenland is changing. It is becoming more modern.

_____ 4. Storms develop over the Atlantic Ocean.

_____ 5. Greenland is fifty times larger than Denmark.

WRITING

Here is a time line of Greenland's history. Look at each date on the time line. Then find what event happened in that year in Greenland and write it next to the date.

3,000 years ago _Eskimos who came from Canada_

875 _Norwegian Vikings were the first Europeans to see the island._

982 _Norwegian Vikings didn't build towns and live there until 982._

1261 _Decided to join the country of Norway_

1380 _Norway united with Denmark_

1814 _Norway ended with Denmark Greenland stayed with Denmark._

WORD STUDY

A. Compound Words

Sometimes you can make a new word by putting two words together. The meaning of the new word is related to the meanings of the two words.

Make compound words from the words in the list. Then choose the best compound word for each sentence.

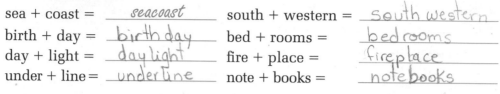

sea + coast = _seacoast_   south + western = _south western_
birth + day = _birth day_   bed + rooms = _bed rooms_
day + light = _day light_   fire + place = _fireplace_
under + line = _underline_   note + books = _notebooks_

1. Dimi was born on October 14. That is his _birthday_.

2. Greenland has 24 hours of _day light_ in the summer. The winter is very dark.

3. Our apartment has two _bedrooms_. I sleep in one, and my parents sleep in the other.

4. Put a line under the answer. _underline_ the answer.

5. We have a _fireplace_ in the living room. In the winter it helps to keep the house warm.

6. The eastern _seacoast_ of Malaysia is very beautiful. People like to go swimming there.

7. In class the students take notes in their _notebooks_.

8. Portugal is in the _southwestern_ part of Europe. It is a beautiful country.

B. Irregular Verbs

Some verbs in English have irregular past-tense forms. Here are some examples.

Present	Past	Past Participle
1. go	went	gone
2. take	took	taken
3. buy	bought	bought
4. cost	cost	cost
5. know	knew	known
6. hear	heard	heard

Choose the correct verb form to complete each sentence. Use a verb from line 1 to sentence 1, and so on.

1. People from Europe _____*went*_____ to live in Greenland.
2. Kiki _____*made*_____ a cake to school last week because it was her birthday.
3. Where did you _____*buy*_____ your new shirt? I really like it.
4. How much did it _____*cost*_____? It looks very expensive.
5. I _____*knew*_____ her phone number yesterday, but today I don't remember it!
6. We _____*heard*_____ some nice music on the radio yesterday.

C. Prepositions

Use the preposition **on**

- to tell the location of something that is touching something else
- with days and dates
- to talk about the radio and TV (television)

Here are some examples:

The book is **on** the table.

The clock is **on** the wall.

Let's play tennis **on** Tuesday.

My part-time job ends **on** January 31.

I listen to the news **on** the radio every morning.

I also watch the news **on** TV every evening.

Complete each sentence with **on, at, to,** or **in.**

1. You can find milk products _____*in*_____ the dairy department.

2. I watched a good program _____*on*_____ television last night.

3. There is another good program _____*at*_____ 8:00 _____*on*_____ Wednesday.

4. Mark bought some new clothes _____*in*_____ the department store ____*in or at*____ the mall.

5. We were _____*at*_____ a party last Friday night until midnight.

6. Please write the answers _____*on*_____ the chalkboard. Then write them _____*in*_____ your notebook.

7. Classes started _____*on*_____ September 11.

8. A very nice painting hangs _____*on*_____ the wall in our classroom.

BUILDING VOCABULARY SKILLS

A. Vocabulary Review

Match the words in column A with their meanings in column B.

A	B
b 1. decide	a. join
e 2. amount	b. choose
d 3. describe	c. think about
c 4. imagine	d. tell about
a 5. connect	e. how much
f 6. last	f. continue

B. Context Clues

You can often understand the meaning of a new word from the other words and information in the sentence or from nearby sentences. The other words that help you understand new words are called **context clues.**

Practice using context clues. Tell the meaning of each word in **bold** print. Use context clues. These words are from Unit 4. (Do not use your dictionary.)

1. What is the **length** of an Olympic stadium?

2. Most of the countries in the world **compete** in the Olympics.

3. **Athletes** practice for a long time before they go to the Olympics.

4. Indonesia, Malaysia, and Japan are all **nations** in the South Pacific Ocean.

5. Several important **events** will take place at my school this week. We have a football game, a picnic, and a test for all the new students.

6. My brother is an **amateur** photographer. He works as an architect, but in his free time he likes to take pictures.

The Olympic Games

1. What are the Olympic Games?
2. Where did they begin?
3. Do you like to watch the Olympics? Why or why not?
4. Name some Olympic sports.

During the Olympic games, people from all over the world come together in peace and friendship. Some of these people compete for medals. Several million people attend the games, and millions of other people watch them on television.

5   Why do we have the Olympic Games? How did they begin? The first Olympic Games that we have records of were in Greece in 776 B.C. The games lasted one day. The only event in the first thirteen Olympic Games was a race. Men ran the length of the stadium (about 192 meters). Then, longer running

races were added. Through the years, a few other kinds of events, like the long
jump, were also added. During this time, the games were for men only, and
women could not even watch them. In the year 393, a Roman emperor ended
the Olympic Games because the quality of the games became very low. The
Olympics did not take place again for 1500 years!

In 1894, Pierre de Coubertin of France helped form the International
Olympic Committee, and the modern Olympic Games began. In 1896 the
games were held again in Athens, Greece. The Greeks built a new stadium for
the competition. Three hundred and eleven athletes from thirteen countries
competed in many events. The winners became national heroes.

After 1896, the games were held every four years during the summer in
different cities around the world. In 1900, the Olympics were in Paris, France,
and women competed for the first time. In 1908, in London, England, the first
gold medals were given to winning athletes. Before that time, the winners
received only silver and bronze medals. The Olympic flag was first introduced
in 1920 in Antwerp, Belgium. The flag has five rings on it. The rings represent
the continents of Africa, Asia, Australia, Europe, and North and South
America. Each ring is a different color—blue, yellow, black, green, or
red—because the flag of each of the countries that compete in the games has at
least one of these colors in it.

The Olympic Winter Games began in 1924 in Chamonix, France. Athletes
competed in winter events such as skiing, ice skating, and ice hockey. Today,
the Winter Games take place every four years. The Summer Games also take
place every four years, but not in the same year as the winter events. Both the
Summer Games and the Winter Games must have at least fifteen events, and
they cannot last more than sixteen days.

Until recently, Olympic competitors could not be professional athletes. All
of the athletes in the Olympic Games were amateurs. Today, however, many of
the Olympic athletes are professionals who play their sports for money during
the year. Some people disagree with this idea. They believe that the Olympic
Games are for amateur athletes, not paid professionals. Other people think
that anyone can play in the Olympic Games. No matter who the athletes are,
millions of people throughout the world enjoy watching the greatest athletic
competitions, the Summer Games and the Winter Games of the Olympics.

WORKING WITH VOCABULARY

A. Focus on the Reading

Choose the best word or phrase for each sentence.

amateurs	compete	event	length
athletes	competition	gold medals	national
attend	competitors	heroes	professionals

1. Several million people __*attend*__ the games, and millions of other people watch them on television.

2. The first Olympic Games were in Greece in 776 B.C. Men ran a footrace the __*length*__ of the stadium (192 meters).

3. In 1896, the games were held again in Athens, Greece. The Greeks built a new stadium for the __*competition*__.

4. Three hundred and eleven __*athletes*__ from thirteen countries competed in many events.

5. The winners became __*national*__ heroes. The people in their countries were very proud of them.

6. In 1908, in London, England, the first __*gold medals*__ were given to the winning athletes.

7. Until recently, Olympic __*competitors*__ could not be professional athletes.

8. All of the athletes in the games were __*amateurs*__. Today, many of the Olympic athletes are __*professionals*__ who play their sports for money during the year.

B. Focus on New Contexts

Choose the best word or phrase for each sentence.

amateur	competition	gold medals	national
athletes	competitors	heroes	professional
compete	event	length	race

1. May 1 is a ___*national*___ holiday in many countries, and people have the day off work.

2. What is the ___*length*___ of a football field? Is it very long?

3. Ice skating is my favorite ___*event*___ in the Winter Games.

4. Jean is a ___*professional*___ photographer. He takes pictures for magazines and newspapers.

5. In the United States, professional ___*athletes*___ are often paid millions of dollars for advertisements.

6. Have you ever heard of a three-legged ___*race*___? Two people run together with one person's leg tied to the other person's leg. It can be very funny!

7. Olympic athletes often become famous in their countries, and children think of them as ___*heroes*___.

8. Do you think that only ___*amateur*___ athletes should compete in the Olympics? Some people think that professional athletes should also be allowed to compete.

UNDERSTANDING THE READING

A. Comprehension Questions

Answer the questions about the reading.

1. What was the only event in the first thirteen Olympic Games?

2. When did the first games begin?

3. Where were the first modern Olympic Games?

4. When were the first Winter Games?

5. How many events must there be in the Winter Games and in the Summer Games?

6. Are Olympic athletes amateurs or professionals?

7. When did women first compete in the Olympics?

*8. When and where are the next Olympic Games?

B. Details

Write **T** if the sentence is true and **F** if it is false.

_T_   1. The first Olympic competitors ran the length of the stadium.

_F_   2. Pierre de Coubertin was an athlete in the first modern games.

_T_   3. Winners have always received gold medals.

_F_   4. The Olympic flag has six colored rings on it.

_F_   5. The summer and winter games take place in the same year.

_T_   6. Today both men and women compete in the Olympics.

_____   *7. Professional athletes make Olympic competition more difficult for amateurs.

C. Main Idea

Check (✔) the three main ideas of the reading.

_____   1. The Olympic Games began in Greece with only one event.

_____   2. The Winter Games and the Summer Games each have at least fifteen events.

_____   3. The Olympics have changed a lot since they began.

_____   4. Skiing is a winter event.

_✓_   5. The Olympic Games bring people together in peace.

WRITING

Write a description of your favorite Olympic event, but do not write the name of the event. Then ask another student to read your description and guess the event. With your partner, try to think of the names of gold-medal winners for the events that you describe.

WORD STUDY

A. Prepositions

Use the preposition **of**

- to show that something belongs to something else (possession)

   the back **of** the car

   the arm **of** the chair

Note: Do not use **of** to show things that belong to people. Instead, use an apostrophe (').

   David**'s** arm

- with numbers

   one **of** the students

   hundreds **of** athletes

- with definite and indefinite amounts of things

   a lot **of** events

   part **of** the team

- to show a relationship between two nouns

   the name **of** the city

   a kind **of** sport

Complete each sentence with **to, in, at,** or **of.**

1. The storm is moving from east _____*to*_____ west.
2. Some _____*of*_____ the Olympic events are very difficult.
3. The first race begins _____*at*_____ 10:00 A.M.
4. The main events are ____*in or at*____ the stadium.
5. Imagine that you are an athlete _____*in*_____ the Olympics.
6. Describe the inside _____*of*_____ the stadium.

7. There are some good athletic shoes on sale _____in_____ the women's department.

8. There are huge containers _____of_____ water for the athletes.

9. Did you read the list _____of_____ competitors for this event?

10. Four _____of_____ the athletes are from South America.

B. Suffixes

Suffixes are endings that we add to words. The suffixes **-al, -able,** and **-ful** can be added to the end of some words. These suffixes mean that something "is full of something" or "has something."

Here are some examples:

The library is a peace**ful** place. (full of peace)

John works in a factory in an industri**al** part of town. (has industry)

This movie theater has very comfort**able** seats. (has comfort)

When you add one of these suffixes to a word, the new word becomes an adjective. An adjective describes a noun or pronoun. It usually comes before a noun or after the verb **be.**

Add suffixes to the following words to make adjectives.

*Spelling Note: Change **y** to **i** before **-al** and **-ful.***

-FUL		-AL		-ABLE	
Noun	**Adjective**	**Noun**	**Adjective**	**Verb**	**Adjective**
beauty	beautiful	coast	coastal	agree	agreeable
help	helpful	nation	national	enjoy	enjoyable
event	eventful	profession	professional	notice	noticeable

Complete each sentence with an adjective from the lists. Then underline the noun or pronoun that it describes.

1. Baseball is a _____national_____ sport in the United States.

2. The first day of the Olympics is an _____eventful_____ day.

3. The change in the weather after a storm is ___enjoyable___. It becomes much cooler.

4. Rita grows ___beautiful___ flowers in her garden.

5. Tariq drinks coffee all day, but his first morning cup of coffee is the most ___enjoyable___ one.

6. Olympic athletes can be amateurs or ___professional___.

7. Mina's directions to her house were very ___helpful___.

8. David is an ___agreeable___ person. He is always very pleasant.

9. Los Angeles is a ___coastal___ city. It is on the Pacific Ocean.

C. Word Forms: Nouns

The direct object of a verb is a noun or a pronoun. The direct object receives the action of the verb. It answers the question "What?"

Look at the example:

Winners receive medals.

What do winners receive? **Medals. Medals** is the direct object.

Sometimes verbs and nouns have the same form. Sometimes we can change adjectives and verbs to nouns by adding a suffix or changing the form of the word. Look at the following nouns. Notice how they are related to other words.

-ITY		-MENT		SAME FORM	
Adjective	**Noun**	**Verb**	**Noun**	**Verb**	**Noun**
nation	nationality	agree	agreement	race	race
electric	electricity	govern	government	ski	ski
able	ability	manage	management	limit	limit
possible	possibility	develop	development	skate	skate

Practice using direct objects. Choose the correct noun form of the word in bold print to complete each sentence.

agree   1. Before you rent an apartment, you have to sign an
               _____ *agreement* _____.

able   2. Some people have a natural ____ ability ____ for
               sports.

race   3. The competitors will run the ____ race ____ at 7:30.

limit   4. The Olympics have a ____ limit ____ of sixteen days.

electric   5. Some small towns and villages do not have
               ____ electricity ____.

manage   6. Helen wants to study hotel ____ management ____ at the
               university.

nation   7. Your passport tells your birth date and your
               ____ nationality ____.

develop   8. Scientists in Greenland watch the ____ development ____ of
               storms over the North Atlantic Ocean.

BUILDING VOCABULARY SKILLS

A. Vocabulary Review

Match the words and phrases in column A with their **opposites** in column B.

A		B	
_c_	1. different	a.	melt
_f_	2. seller	b.	traditional
_d_	3. take apart	c.	similar
_e_	4. very small	d.	connect
_b_	5. modern	e.	huge
_a_	6. freeze	f.	customer
_h_	7. work hard	g.	major
_g_	8. not important	h.	relax

B. Context Clues

Choose the answer that is closest in meaning to each word in bold print. Use context clues.

1. There is a fire in the building! You must leave **immediately!**
   a. soon
   b. right now
   c. in a few minutes
   d. in a little while

2. Japan has a lot of **factories.** They make cars, televisions, and computers.
   a. jobs
   b. schools
   c. buildings where they sell things
   d. buildings where they make things

3. Some clothing factories make shirts. Workers **dye** the shirts different colors.
   a. color
   b. change
   c. wear
   d. sell

4. Many people moved to San Francisco in the 1800s to work in the **gold mines.** They worked very hard digging for gold in the mountains.
   a. stores
   b. factories
   c. places where people sell gold
   d. places where people work to find gold

5. Some boats have **sails.** The wind blows the sails and moves these boats. They do not need engines.
   a. large motors
   b. two small pieces of wood
   c. huge pieces of strong cloth
   d. small motors outside a boat

6. When I was a student I lived with my parents. Now I have my own apartment and a job. I am **independent.**
   a. alone
   b. not able to live alone
   c. able to live and work without help
   d. not able to find a job or an apartment

Pre-reading

1. Do you wear jeans? When?
2. Why are blue jeans popular?
3. Where do jeans come from?

Jeans are the most popular kind of clothing in the world. Millions and millions of jeans are sold each year. They are popular almost everywhere—in Asia, Europe, North and South America, Australia, and Africa. All kinds of people wear jeans. Jeans come in many colors and styles. They can be very expensive or inexpensive. Some people wear jeans everywhere they go! Why are jeans so popular in the world? Where did blue jeans come from?

In 1847, a man named Levi Strauss moved to the United States from Bavaria (now part of Germany). He went to New York to work with his brothers at their store. After a few years there, he decided to move west to

5

10 California. Many people, hoping to become rich, moved west at that time to work in the gold mines. Levi Strauss moved to San Francisco in 1853 and started a business selling supplies to the miners. He called the business Levi Strauss & Company. One day, in 1872, a man wrote Levi Strauss a letter. The man's name was Jacob Davis. He suggested that Levi make pants with strong

15 seams for miners, because working the mines was very difficult. He said that putting metal rivets on the pockets would make them very strong. Levi liked the idea and hired the man.

Levi Strauss and his partner needed a strong fabric, or cloth, to make clothing from. They found a very strong cloth from Nimes, France. It was the

20 right fabric for strong work pants. Levi Strauss used it to make pants for the California gold miners. The fabric became known as *de Nimes* (from Nimes), or *denim.* Levi Strauss took the denim and dyed it blue with indigo. Indigo is the oldest natural dye in the world. The blue denim pants immediately became popular with the miners.

25 Denim was also a popular material in Europe in the fifteenth century. Because it was so strong, people used it to make sails for ships. Some people say that Christopher Columbus used denim sails when he came to America.

Today Levi Strauss & Company makes jeans in large factories. It also makes other clothing, such as jackets and shirts. Almost everything made of denim is

30 very popular. Jeans today come in many different colors. There are black jeans, green jeans, and even red jeans. The most popular color of all is still blue. People wear blue jeans to work, to school, to parties, and just to relax. They wear jeans with holes in them. They cut off the legs and wear them as shorts. People

35 wear jeans any way they like.

Why are jeans so popular? In the United States, they are the only kind of traditional American clothing. In other

40 countries, young people wear them because they want to look modern. Jeans are a sign of youth and independence. People like to feel modern, young, and

45 independent.

WORKING WITH VOCABULARY

A. Focus on the Reading

Choose the best word for each sentence.

denim	immediately	miners	sails
dye	independence	popular	strong
factories	indigo	rivets	youth

1. Levi Strauss moved to San Francisco in 1853 and started a business selling supplies to the _miners_ .

2. Jacob Davis suggested that Levi Strauss make pants with _strong_ seams for the miners.

3. The fabric became known as *de Nimes* (from Nimes), or _denim_ .

4. Levi Strauss took the denim and dyed it blue with _indigo_ .

5. Indigo is the oldest natural _dye_ in the world.

6. Because denim was so strong, people used it to make _sails_ for ships.

7. Today Levi Strauss & Company makes jeans in large _factories_ .

8. Jeans are a sign of _youth_ and _independence_ .

B. Focus on New Contexts

Choose the best word for each sentence.

denim	immediately	miners	sails
dye	independence	popular	strong
factories	indigo	rivets _remache_	youth

1. Today, jackets, shirts, and many other kinds of clothing are made from _denim_ .

2. ___Indigo___ is a very dark blue color. It is one of the colors of the rainbow.

3. Joong made a sturdy bookcase for his books. He used some long pieces of wood and metal _____.

4. The ___factories___ create a lot of pollution in this area.

5. What kind of music is ___popular___ with young people today?

6. We are really late. If we don't leave ___immediately___, we will miss our plane.

7. Some people like to ___dye___ their hair a different color, like blonde.

8. The young people, or the ___youth___, of a country usually have their own special styles or fashions. What's popular with young people in your country now?

UNDERSTANDING THE READING

A. Comprehension Questions

Answer the questions about the reading.

1. Why are jeans popular everywhere?
2. Who made the first jeans?
3. Why did they put rivets on the seams of jeans?
4. What kind of cloth did they use for the miners' jeans?
*5. What kind of cloth do factories use today to make jeans?
*6. Do older people like jeans? Why or why not?
7. What other products are made of denim?

B. Details

Circle the letter of the best answer.

1. The word *denim* comes from the name of a city in
   a. France.
   b. Bavaria.
   c. Germany.
   d. the United States.

2. Levi Strauss went to California
    a. to look for gold.
    b. to make jeans.
    c. to work with his brothers.
    d. to sell supplies to the miners.

3. Rivets
    a. make good sails.
    b. make pockets strong.
    c. are made of denim.
    d. come from France.

4. Jacob Davis
    a. worked in France.
    b. made jeans before Levi Strauss.
    c. wrote a letter to Levi Strauss.
    d. came from New York.

5. Today jeans
    a. are not made of denim.
    b. come in many different colors.
    c. are only popular with miners.
    d. are only worn in America.

C. Main Idea

Check (✔) the two main ideas of the reading.

_____ 1. Many people moved to California to look for gold.

_____ 2. Levi Strauss introduced jeans to the United States.

_____ 3. Indigo is a blue dye.

_____ 4. Today jeans are popular all over the world.

_____ 5. The word denim comes from the name of a city in France.

WRITING

Jeans are in fashion almost everywhere, especially with young people. What else is popular in your country these days? Make a list of the things people wear or do to show that they are young and modern. Compare your list with your classmates' lists.

WORD STUDY

A. Word Forms: Nouns

Some nouns that end in **-th** or **-ght** are related to similar words that are not nouns. Read the following pairs of sentences and see how the words in bold print are related.

a. An Olympic stadium is very **long.** In the first Olympics, people ran a race the **length** of the stadium.

b. George is very **strong.** He has a lot of **strength** in his arms.

c. My street is twenty meters **wide.** Its **width** is twenty meters.

d. Some plants **grow** very quickly. Their **growth** is fast.

e. That river is fifteen meters **deep.** Its **depth** is fifteen meters.

f. How **high** is that mountain? What is its **height?**

g. How much do you **weigh?** What is your **weight?**

Now choose the best word for each sentence.

growth	depth	strength	length
width ✔	height	weight	

1. What is the _____*width*_____ of this room? Is it wide enough for ten chairs?

2. Rivets made jeans stronger. They gave ___*strength*___ to the jeans.

3. What is the ___*length*___ of this bridge? It looks very long.

4. The ceilings in this old apartment are very high. Do you know their ___*height*___ .

5. How deep is the Panama Canal. What is its ___depth___?

6. This year I grew tomato plants in my backyard. I was surprised by their ___growth___ .

7. Anne is much thinner now. She weighs 125 pounds. She lost a lot of ___weight___ .

B. Prepositions

The preposition **by** means "near" or "along."

Look at these examples:

> The teacher is standing **by** the desk.

> I walked **by** the library on my way to class today.

By is also used with time, when you want to show that something should happen *before* or *not later than* a certain time.

Look at this example:

> We need to leave at 7:30, so if you want to come with us, please be here by 7:25.

Complete each sentence with **at, by, in, of, to,** or **on.**

1. Rome is one ___of___ the most beautiful cities in the world.

2. The telephone is ___by___ the computer ___on___ the desk.

3. You must be ___at___ the airport ___by___ 5:30. Your plane leaves at 6:00, and you must be there thirty minutes early.

4. Your seat is ___by___ the window. My seat is ___on___ the aisle.

5. Let's drive ___by___ the new mall on the way home. We don't have time to stop, but we can look ___at___ it as we drive ___by___ .

6. Mark's father works _____*in*_____ the meat department

_____*at*_____ the supermarket.

7. I thought that I left my gloves _____*on*_____ my desk

_____*by*_____ my books, but now I can't find them.

8. Sarah likes to take long walks _____*to, by*_____ the river in the

summer.

C. Irregular Verbs

Some verbs have irregular past tense forms. Study the verbs in this chart. Then choose the correct form to complete each sentence. Use a verb from line 1 for sentence 1, and so on.

Present	Past	Past Participle
1. put	put	put
2. let	let	let
3. pay	paid	paid
4. find	found	found
5. sell	sold	sold
6. meet	met	met

1. My freezer doesn't work. If I _____*put*_____ ice cream in it, the ice cream melts.

2. Parents usually don't _____*let*_____ their children go out alone late at night.

3. Tom bought a new pair of jeans. They look very expensive. I think he _____*paid*_____ a lot of money for them.

4. I lost my favorite pen yesterday. I can't _____*find*_____ it anywhere.

5. Michael wanted a new bicycle, so he _____*sold*_____ his old one and bought a new one.

6. I _____*met*_____ a lot of nice people in my English class last year.

BUILDING VOCABULARY SKILLS

A. Vocabulary Review

Match the words in column A with their meanings in column B.

A	B
c 1. on sale	a. but
e 2. unite	b. reach
b 3. stretch	c. at a cheaper price
a 4. however	d. giving and getting information
d 5. communication	e. join together
g 6. immediately	f. part of a ship
f 7. sails	g. right now

B. Context Clues

Tell the meaning of each word in bold print.

1. If you **grind** corn into powder, you can cook with it. *(moler o afilar)*

2. Buddhism and Christianity are two of the world's **religions.**

3. A carpenter uses nails and **glue** to put furniture together.

4. You can see many famous paintings in an art **museum.**

5. Bill has a very good job. He **earns** a lot of money, and he really likes his work.

6. Some farmers grow vegetables and also **raise** animals.

7. In Greenland, people wear warm clothing made of **wool.** *(lana)*

Navajo Sand Painting

Pre-reading

1. What do you know about Native American Indians?
2. What kind of Indian art have you seen?
3. Are there any traditional ceremonies using art in your culture? Explain.

~~Indian~~
Native Americans

The Navajo Indians live in the American Southwest. This is a desert area, dry and sandy with few plants. It is generally flat in the desert, but some great mountains rise up against the sky. This area is very colorful because of the minerals in the sand. The desert sand is a mixture of red, gold, and white. The
5   nights are very dark, and the sky is full of stars. The Southwest is a beautiful part of the United States.

    The Navajos came to what is now the southwestern part of the United States from the areas that are now Canada and Alaska about 500 years ago. Now they live in reservation communities in Arizona, New Mexico, and Utah.

10   Reservations are special areas of land that the U.S. government has set aside
     for Indian communities. The Navajos have very strong traditions from
     centuries ago. One of these traditions is called sand painting.
        The Navajos use sand paintings as part of their religion. Sand painting is a
     ceremony for helping sick people. The people in Navajo communities who
15   make sand paintings are called singers, or medicine men. Singers are special
     people. They are the only ones who are allowed to create sand paintings.
     First, a singer collects rocks of several different colors. Then he grinds them
     into sand. This is what he will use for the painting.
        The singer always makes the painting on the floor of a small Navajo house.
20   He takes some colored sand in his hand and puts it on the floor in a line.
     He works with different colors and slowly makes a picture. The sick person
     sits in the center of the sand painting. Navajos believe that when the picture
     is finished, the person's sickness goes into the picture. They also believe
     that when the medicine man erases the picture from the floor, the sickness
25   goes too.
        A Navajo singer learns his art from an older singer. All medicine men make
     their sand paintings from memory. A singer always makes the same kind of
     picture in exactly the same way. Because it takes many years to learn the art of
     sand painting, very few young people are singers.
30   Navajos have always welcomed new ideas. They got sheep, horses, and
     cows from the Spanish. They used the wool from their sheep to make
     beautiful rugs. In the 1880s, they started using some of the pictures from sand
     paintings in their rug designs. The pictures were similar to the original ones,
     but they were not exactly the same. The Navajo artists always changed a color
35   or a line. They would not use their religious pictures without changing them a
     little.
        In the 1930s, the Navajos started making sand paintings to sell. They put
     the paintings on a board with glue and sold the paintings to tourists. However,
     the pictures were always a little different from the original pictures.
40   Most Navajo Indians today have difficult lives. They still raise sheep, but
     farming is difficult because the land is very dry. They have no factories, and it
     is not easy to find a job. They can earn a lot of money by selling their sand
     paintings. Navajos still use sand paintings for their religious ceremonies.
     However, the singer, or medicine man, never makes paintings to sell.
45   Business and religion are always separate. Some Navajos think that they

should not sell sand paintings to tourists. Others think that it is a good way to earn money.

Before 1930, no one except Navajo Indians could see their beautiful sand paintings. Now everyone can see them in museums or buy them in art
50 galleries.

WORKING WITH VOCABULARY

A. Focus on the Reading

Choose the best word for each sentence.

board	glue	painting	separate
earn	grinds	raise	sickness
exactly	museums	religion	wool

1. The Navajos have very strong traditions from centuries ago. One of these traditions is called sand _painting_.

2. First the singer collects rocks of several different colors. Then he _grinds_ them into sand.

3. Navajos believe that when the picture is finished, the person's _sickness_ goes into the picture.

4. The Navajos used the _wool_ from their sheep to make beautiful rugs.

5. The pictures in the rugs were similar to the original ones, but they were not _exactly_ the same.

6. In the 1930s, the Navajos started making sand paintings to sell. They put the paintings on a _board_ with _glue_ and sold the paintings to tourists.

7. Most Navajo Indians today have difficult lives. They still _raise_ sheep, but farming is difficult because the land is very dry.

8. Business and religion are always _separate_.

B. Focus on New Contexts

Choose the best word for each sentence.

board	glue	painting	separate
earn	grind	raises	sickness
exactly	museums	religions	wool

1. It is hard to _____earn_____ money as a farmer in a very dry country.

2. Today people can see many examples of Native American Indian art in _____museums_____ all around the United States.

3. I need to buy a heavy _____wool_____ coat to wear this winter.

4. My cousin has a farm. She _____raises_____ sheep and cows.

5. Children use paper and _____glue_____ in art class at school.

6. In the United States, government and religion are _____separate_____. They cannot be together. It is a law.

7. Islam, Judaism, and Christianity are very old _____religions_____. They began thousands and thousands of years ago.

8. American English and British English are very similar, but they are not _____exactly_____ the same. Some words are different.

UNDERSTANDING THE READING

A. Comprehension Questions

Answer the questions about the reading.

1. Why do the Navajo Indians make sand paintings?

2. Where does a Navajo medicine man get the sand for his painting?

3. Where does he make the painting?

4. How do people learn to become singers?

5. What did the Navajos get from the Spanish?

6. Why did they start making sand paintings on boards?

7. Why do they always change the picture a little?

8. Why do the Navajos disagree about selling their sand paintings?

B. Details

Write **T** if the sentence is true and **F** if it is false. Write **NI** if there is not enough information in the reading to answer true or false.

T 1. Sand paintings are part of the Navajo religion.

F 2. The Navajos made wool rugs before the Spanish came to America.

T 3. Navajos earn a lot of money from their rugs.

F 4. Any Navajo can make religious sand paintings.

F 5. Pictures used in Navajo rug designs are exactly like religious sand paintings.

T 6. Navajos have strong traditions.

F 7. Navajos make their own glue.

C. Main Idea

Check (✔) the three main ideas of the reading.

✔ 1. The American Southwest has many beautiful rocks.

___ 2. Navajos use sand paintings for their religion and to earn money.

___ 3. Navajos make rugs to sell to tourists.

___ 4. Sand painting is an old and important Navajo ceremony.

___ 5. Life for the Navajos is difficult.

WRITING

Every culture has its own kinds of art. What is a traditional art in your culture? Write a paragraph about a traditional art from your culture. If you can, also bring a picture to class to show an example of this kind of art. When you finish, exchange paragraphs with a partner.

WORD STUDY

A. Word Forms: Pronouns

Pronouns that end in **-self** or **-selves** are called reflexive pronouns. A reflexive pronoun refers to the subject of the sentence.

Look at these example sentences:

I live by **myself.**

You must remind **yourself** to finish your homework.

Monica is a wonderful cook. She made a huge dinner by **herself.**

Charlie is very independent. He prefers to work by **himself.**

A baby bird cannot feed **itself.** It needs help from its mother.

My sister and I don't live with our parents. We have an apartment by **ourselves.**

Can you and Michael take the bus by **yourselves,** or do you want a ride?

My neighbors don't go to school to learn English. They are teaching **themselves** at home.

Complete each sentence with the correct reflexive pronoun.

1. When you want to remember something, say it out loud to _____ *yourself* _____.

2. I don't make my clothes _____ myself _____. I buy them.

3. We cannot finish our homework by _____ ourselves _____. We have to do it in class.

4. A baby cat cannot find food for _____ itself _____.

5. Kim doesn't usually eat in the cafeteria. She prefers to cook for _____ herself _____.

6. If you speak English among _____ yourselves _____, you will learn faster.

7. Amateur athletes often learn a sport by _____ themselves _____.

8. Pierre learned English by _____ himself _____. He did not study in a class.

B. Word Forms: Nouns and Verbs

Sometimes in English we can change an adjective to a noun by adding a suffix or changing the spelling.

Look at the examples. Complete the chart.

*Spelling Note: Change **y** to **i** before adding **-ness**.*

-NESS		T→CE	
Adjective	**Noun**	**Adjective**	**Noun**
sick	sickness	independent	independence
happy	*happiness*	important	*importance*
		different	*difference*

We can change some nouns and adjectives into verbs by adding the suffix **-en.** For example, if you add **-en** to the adjective **bright,** you get the word **brighten. Brighten** means "to make something bright."

Look at these examples. Complete the chart.

Adjective	**Verb**	**Noun**	**Verb**
dark	darken	strength	strengthen
wide	*widen*	length	*lengthen*
short	*shorten*		

Complete each sentence with the correct form of the word in bold print.

independent
1. Jeans are a sign of youth and _*independence*_.

strength
2. Levi Strauss used rivets to _*strengthen*_ the pockets on his jeans.

happy
3. All people want to find peace and _*happiness*_ in their lives.

dark
4. If you add a little black paint to the blue it will _*darken*_ it.

sick

5. The Navajos believe that when the medicine man erases the sand painting, the person's ___sickness___ goes away.

wide

6. My street is too narrow. I wish they would ___widen___ it.

important

7. Athletes know the ___importance___ of practicing every day.

length

8. My pants are too short. I need to ___lengthen___ them.

different

9. Is there a ___difference___ between Canadian English and American English?

short

10. That dress is too long. If you ___shorten___ it just a little, it will be the perfect length.

BUILDING VOCABULARY SKILLS

A. Vocabulary Review

Choose five words from this list and make a sentence with each one.

mind	amount	container	medals
sheet	dial	compete	immediately

1. Please Mary lend me a sheet of paper.
2. My family is in my mind always.
3. Raquel had an accident. Immediately I called to the ambulance.
4. Maribel dial the number from the hotel at the airport
5. My cousin has a lot of medals.

B. Context Clues

Choose the answer that is closest in meaning to each word in bold print. Use context clues.

1. Wool comes from sheep. We make clothes from it. Most **leather** comes from cows. We use it to make shoes and bags.
   a. something to eat
   c. something made from animal skin
   b. something to drink
   d. something made from animal hair

2. Marconi **invented** the radio. Bell **invented** the telephone.
   a. used
   c. found
   b. liked
   d. made the first one

3. I have an important **message** for you. Your family phoned and you must call them back immediately.
   a. book
   c. picture
   b. medal
   d. communication

4. A special **exhibit** of Indian art opens at the National Museum this month. I want to see it.
   a. sand
   c. music
   b. show
   d. go out

5. The army sends its messages in **code** so no one else can understand them.
   a. letters
   c. a secret way to communicate
   b. by telephone
   d. a modern way to communicate

6. Let's have the test on Monday **instead of** Friday so we can study this weekend.
   a. with
   c. in place of
   b. besides
   d. in back of

colors
colour

Unit 7 Braille

Pre-reading

1. How do people who cannot see read books and signs?
2. What is Braille?
3. Where do you find signs in Braille?

Louis Braille was born in 1809 in a small town in France. His father had a small business. He made shoes and other things from leather. Louis liked to help his father in the store. One day when Louis was three years old, he was cutting some leather. Suddenly the knife slipped and hit him in the eye. Soon
5 Louis could not see at all.

At first Louis went to school in his village with other children who were not visually impaired. The children at this school could see. They had normal eyesight. He understood immediately that it was very important for people to learn how to read. He also understood that visually impaired people needed a

10 special way to read. When he was ten years old, Louis went to Paris to study at the National Institute for the Blind, a special school for visually impaired students. There he found huge books with large, raised letters. Students tried to read by feeling the big letters. Louis decided to find a better way for visually impaired people to read.

15 One day Louis went with his class to a special exhibit by a captain in the army. One thing in this exhibit was very interesting to Louis. The captain showed him a special code he had made. The army used this code to send messages at night. People in the army wrote this code in raised marks on very thick paper.

20 Louis thought a lot about this code. Then he decided to write his own code so visually impaired people could read with their fingers. Louis found that it was very difficult to feel the difference between raised letters. Instead of letters, Louis used a system of raised dots. He arranged them in a "cell" of six dots, with two dots across and three down.

25 With his cell of dots, Louis could make sixty-three different combinations. Each combination, or arrangement, stands for one letter, punctuation mark, or number. Louis invented this system when he was only fifteen years old. It is called the Braille system. Visually impaired people can read by feeling the raised dots with their fingers. They know what letters the dots represent.

30 Today Braille books are found in all written languages in the world. In many countries you can find signs in Braille in elevators and in buildings such as hospitals. People can also write in Braille. There are special pens, typewriters, and computers for Braille.

Louis Braille invented a way for visually impaired people to communicate
35 through reading and writing. When he died in 1852, he was buried in the Pantheon in Paris. Only national heroes of France are buried in this place, and Louis Braille was a national hero.

WORKING WITH VOCABULARY

A. Focus on the Reading

Choose the best word or phrase for each sentence.

arranged	combinations	instead of	messages
buried	exhibit	invented	slipped
code	impaired	leather	system

1. Louis Braille's father had a small business. He made shoes and other things from _leather_.

2. One day when Louis was only three years old, he was cutting some leather. Suddenly the knife _slipped_ and hit him in the eye.

3. At first Louis went to school in his village with other children who were not visually _impaired_. The children at this school could see. They had normal eyesight.

4. One day Louis went with his class to a special _exhibit_ by a captain in the army.

5. The captain showed him a special _code_ that he used to send _messages_.

6. _Instead of_ letters, Louis used a system of raised dots.

7. He _arranged_ them in a cell of six dots, with two dots across and three down.

8. With his cell of dots, Louis could make sixty-three different _combinations_.

9. Louis _invented_ this system when he was only fifteen years old.

10. When he died in 1852, he was _buried_ in the Pantheon in Paris.

B. Focus on New Contexts

Choose the best word or phrase for each sentence.

arrange	combination	instead of	message
buried	exhibit	invented	slipped
code	impaired	leather	system

1. The metric _____*system*_____ of measurement is used all over the world.

2. Some visually _____*impaired*_____ people have specially trained dogs who walk with them and help them.

3. A special _____*exhibit*_____ of Chinese art opens at the museum this month.

4. Last winter Michael _____*slipped*_____ on the ice and broke his arm.

5. I saw a beautiful _____*leather*_____ coat at the store yesterday. I would like to buy it.

6. I'm tired of going to the library. Let's study at my apartment _____*instead of*_____ the library today.

7. If we _____*arrange*_____ the chairs in the classroom in a circle we can all see each other better.

8. When kings died in ancient Egypt, they were _____*buried*_____ with treasures like gold, silver, and jewels.

UNDERSTANDING THE READING

A. Comprehension Questions

Answer the questions about the reading.

1. What was Louis Braille's nationality?

2. How did he lose his eyesight?

3. What gave him the idea for the Braille system?

4. How old was he when he invented the system?

5. How do visually impaired people use the Braille system?

6. Where was Louis Braille buried?

B. Details

Circle the letter of the best answer.

1. Louis Braille's father made things from
   a. codes.
   b. wool.
   c. leather.
   d. exhibit.

2. When Louis was ten years old, he began to study
   a. at a university.
   b. in the army.
   c. at his neighborhood school.
   d. at a special school for the visually impaired.

3. Louis saw a special exhibit by an army captain. The captain showed Louis
   a. a code he made.
   b. a special book.
   c. an art exhibit.
   d. a system of raised letters.

4. Louis found that it was difficult to feel the differences between
   a. codes.
   b. raised letters.
   c. different languages.
   d. arrangements of dots.

5. Louis invented a system
   a. for army captains.
   b. of raised dots.
   c. of very big letters.
   d. for French heroes.

6. With his cell of dots, Louis could
   a. make sixty-three different combinations.
   b. send messages.
   c. work in the army.
   d. make raised letters.

C. Main Idea

Check (✔) the main idea of the reading.

_____ 1. Louis Braille visited an exhibit of codes.

___✓___ 2. Louis Braille invented a system of reading for visually impaired people.

_____ 3. Louis Braille didn't like the raised letters.

_____ 4. Louis Braille was buried in the Pantheon.

WRITING

Here is the Braille alphabet. Each combination of dots represents a letter, a pair of letters often found together, or a very common short word. Write a message in Braille on a piece of paper. Then exchange your paper with another student and try to read the code! Remember, you can see the code, but visually impaired people can only feel it.

A	B	C	D	E	F	G	H	I	J

K	L	M	N	O	P	Q	R	S	T

U	V	X	Y	Z	and	for	of	the	with

ch	gh	sh	th	wh	ed	er	ou	ow	w

WORD STUDY

A. Word Forms: Nouns

In English, a preposition is usually followed by a noun.

Look at the examples:

> I will meet you **at school.**
>
> Marco bought this gift **for your sister.**
>
> Can you give it **to her?**

When we add a suffix to some verbs, we can make nouns. Sometimes a verb and a noun have the same form.

Look at these examples:

-TURE		-OR		SAME FORM	
Verb	**Noun**	**Verb**	**Noun**	**Verb**	**Noun**
furnish	furniture	sail	sailor	sail	sail
sign	signature	invent	inventor	change	change
		compete	competitor	start	start

Practice using nouns and prepositions. Complete each sentence with the noun form of the word in bold. Circle the prepositions that you know.

compete   1. (In) the Olympics, the gold medal is (for) the best
_____*competitor*_____ .

furnish   2. What kind of ___*furniture*___ do you like best? I like modern things, but my sister likes antiques.

change   3. We will have class in the library tomorrow. Please tell the other students about this ___*change*___ .

start   4. The athletes are getting ready for the ___*start*___ of the race.

sail   5. The ship's captain talked to a ___*sailor*___ about the weather at sea.

sign   6. Write your _signature_ on this line for your visa application.

invent   7. Do you know what other useful things were made by the _inventor_ of the electric light bulb, Thomas Edison?

sail   8. The sailboat stopped moving because the storm made a big hole in the _sail_.

B. Irregular Verbs

Some verbs in English have irregular past forms.

Here are some examples:

Present	Past	Past Participle
1. see	saw	seen
2. have	had	had
3. say	said	said
4. tell	told	told
5. lose	lost	lost
6. build	built	built
7. grind	ground	ground

Choose the correct verb form to complete the paragraph. Use a verb from line 1 for sentence 1, and so on.

Have you ever (1) _seen_ a Navajo sand painting? I (2) _had_, and they are very beautiful. I visited Arizona last summer and met some Navajo artists. Navajos (3) _said_ that only special people, called singers, can make these beautiful, religious paintings. One old singer (4) _told_ me that it takes years and years of study to create these special paintings. He hopes that more young Navajos will study and learn how to make these designs. If they don't learn soon, the traditional Navajo art will be (5) _lost_. Some Navajos make sand paintings to sell to tourists. They are not religious paintings, and they are not made by singers. I met one man who

(6) _____*built*_____ a small art gallery to sell traditional Indian art. He also makes sand paintings himself. First he finds some colored rocks. Then he (7) _____*ground*_____ the rocks into sand and makes designs with it on a board. His paintings are so beautiful! I bought one as a present for my friend's birthday.

BUILDING VOCABULARY SKILLS

A. Vocabulary Review

Circle the word that does not belong with the other words. Tell why the other three words go together.

1. miner, sailor, competitor, event
2. sand, denim, wool, leather
3. glue, sand, medal, board
4. musem, communication, supermarket, factory
5. long, width, depth, height
6. seacoast, underline, amateur, notebook
7. inexpensive, dishonest, unsafe, beautiful

B Context Clues

Tell the meaning of each word in bold print. Use context clues.

1. The **population** of China is more than one billion.
2. Kathleen is doing **research** for her Ph.D. in engineering. She looks for information in books and journals in the library. Then she will write a very long paper.
3. Marco likes to read scientific **journals.** He buys two or three every week and reads articles about new discoveries in science around the world.
4. Some flowers are made of plastic. They can never die because they are **artificial.**
5. India was a **colony** of England. Vietnam was a **colony** of France. Mexico was a **colony** of Spain.

6. **Even though** he didn't study, John got a high score on the test. He is very smart.

7. If you are flying from London to Paris, you must go to the **international** terminal at the airport. Flights within England leave from the domestic terminal.

English, the International Language

Pre-reading

1. Where is English used in your country?
2. What language do most people learn as a second language?
3. Why do so many people learn to speak English?

More than 6,000 languages are spoken in the world today. Of course, many of these languages are spoken by small groups of people. In fact, some languages are spoken by only a few hundred people. On the other hand, more than 200 languages are spoken by groups of one million or more people. Of

5   these languages, 24 have more than 50 million speakers each. Many people all over the world use one international language to communicate with each other. That language is English.

    More than 400 million people speak English as their first, or native, language. Yet there are now even more speakers of English as a second

10 language than there are speakers of English as a first language! The number of
people who speak English is growing quickly. Because of the huge population
of China—more than one billion people—Chinese is the only language with
more speakers than English.

English is the native or official language of one-fifth of the land area of the
15 world. It is spoken in Australia, Canada, Great Britain, Ireland, New Zealand,
South Africa, and the United States. It is also one of the official languages in
India.

More people study English than any other language. In many countries, the
textbooks in universities are in English. Furthermore, many university classes
20 are taught in English even though English is not the native language of the
students.

English is the language of international communication. It is the language
of international business, research, and science. More than three-fourths of
the world's mail is written in English. Three-fifths of the world's radio stations
25 use English. More than half of the world's scientific and research journals are
in English. Most other languages have borrowed many English words.

Why did English become the international language? In the middle of the
nineteenth century, French was the international language. Then England
became very powerful in the world. England started colonies in North
30 America and India and, later, in Asia, Africa, and the South Pacific. The
people in those colonies had to use English. Slowly, it became more useful
and important internationally than French. After the Second World War, the
United States became very powerful, and even more people began to learn
English.

35 Is English a good international language? It is probably the world's largest
language with more than one million words! The grammar is simpler than in
the other major languages. However, English spelling is difficult, especially
for nonnative speakers of English. The major reason that spelling in English
is difficult is that Modern English spelling represents Old English
40 pronunciation. The English we use today is written almost the same as it was
hundreds and hundreds of years ago, but the way people pronounce the
words has changed a lot. Therefore, many words in English are not
pronounced the way they are spelled.

People have often tried to create new languages for communication.
45 Hundreds of artificial languages have been invented since 1880. *Esperanto* is

the most well-known of these "universal" languages. No one speaks these languages as a native language. People try to use them to communicate in the world. However, none of them has ever become very popular. English is the only true international language.

WORKING WITH VOCABULARY

A. Focus on the Reading

Choose the best word or phrase for each sentence.

area	even though	native	powerful
artificial	international	official	research
colonies	journals	population	simpler

1. Many people all over the world use one _international_ language to communicate with each other. That language is English.

2. Because of the huge _population_ of China—more than one billion people—Chinese is the only language with more speakers than English.

3. English is the native or _official_ language of one-fifth of the land _area_ of the world.

4. Many university classes are taught in English _even though_ English is not the native language of the students.

5. English is the language of international communication. It is the language of international business, _research_ , and science.

6. More than half of the world's scientific and research _journals_ are in English.

7. In the middle of the nineteenth century, French was the international language. Then England became very _powerful_ in the world.

8. England started _colonies_ in North America and India and, later, in Asia, Africa, and the South Pacific.

9. Is English a good international language? The grammar is
   simpler than in the other major languages.
   However, English spelling is difficult.

10. People have often tried to create new languages for communication.
    Hundreds of _artificial_ languages have been invented
    since 1880.

B. Focus on New Contexts

Choose the best word or phrase for each sentence.

area	even though	native	powerful
artificial	international	official	research
colonies	journals	population	simpler

1. Did you know that Portuguese is the _native_ language of
   people from Brazil?

2. Robert's new apartment is in a beautiful _area_. Across the
   street from his building is a little park with many trees and flowers.

3. Do you know the names of the original thirteen _colonies_ that
   became the United States?

4. Everyone had a wonderful time at the class picnic _even though_ it
   rained all afternoon.

5. You must know English if you want to do scientific _research_
   at a university.

6. Those flowers are beautiful! Are they real or _artificial_? I can't
   tell!

7. The United States of Mexico is the _official_ name of Mexico.

UNDERSTANDING THE READING

A. Comprehension Questions

Answer the questions about the reading.

*1. Are Japanese and Arabic each spoken by more than 50 million people?

2. How many languages have more than one million speakers?

3. How many people speak English as a native language?

4. What language has the most speakers? Why?

*5. Why do some countries use English textbooks even though English is not the native language?

*6. Why are scientific journals usually written in English?

7. Why did English become the international language?

8. What is an artificial language?

B. Details

Circle the letter of the best answer.

1. China has a population of more than
   a. one thousand.   c. one billion.
   b. one million.   d. one trillion.

*2. English is the native language of people in
   a. Africa.   c. all of Canada.
   b. Australia.   d. Malaysia.

3. Three-fifths of the world's
   a. population speaks English.
   b. mail is in English.
   c. radio stations use English.
   d. scientific journals are in English.

4. English spelling is
   a. easy.   c. simple.
   b. fun.   d. difficult.

5. Modern English spelling represents

   a. Modern English pronunciation.

   (b.) Old English pronunciation.

   c. how powerful England was.

   d. how simple the grammar is.

6. Artificial languages are spoken as native languages

   (a.) by no one. c. by people who speak English.

   b. by people all over the world. d. in the South Pacific.

C. Main Idea

Check (✔) the main idea of the reading.

_____ 1. French was the international language around 1850.

✓ 2. English is the major international language of the world.

_____ 3. English is used in many universities.

_____ 4. Nonnative speakers of English think that English is simple.

WRITING

What are some of the major differences between your native language and English? Make a list of some of the differences. Then discuss them with a partner.

WORD STUDY

A. Word Forms: Past Participles as Adjectives

The past participle form of a verb can be used as an adjective. The past participles of regular verbs end in **-ed.** They are the same as the past tense forms. Irregular verbs have irregular past participles.

Look at these examples:

Because I work, I have only **limited** time to study.

Spoken English is easier than **written** English.

Here are some irregular verbs to learn.

Present	Past	Past Participle
eat	ate	eaten
speak	spoke	spoken
write	wrote	written
make	made	made
limit	limited	limited
know	knew	known

Now complete each sentence with the correct past participle. In these sentences, the past participle forms are used as adjectives. Circle the noun it describes.

1. Some languages are _____*written*_____ (languages) only. No one speaks them.
2. Chinese and English are ____*spoken*____ languages.
3. Some languages have a ____*limited*____ vocabulary, but English has more than one million words.
4. This sweater was <u>hand</u> ____*made*____ by my grandmother.
5. Last night I did not feel well. I left my dinner <u>un</u>____*eaten*____.
6. Muhammad Ali was a well-____*Known*____ boxer.

B. Irregular Verbs

Study the verbs in the chart. Then choose the best verb form to complete each sentence. Use a verb from line 1 for sentence 1, and so on.

Present	Past	Past Participle
1. get	got	gotten
2. forget	forgot	forgotten
3. stand	stood	stood
4. understand	understood	understood
5. come	came	come
6. become	became	become
7. run	ran	run
8. begin	began	begun

1. I _____*got*_____ two letters this week. One was from my mother, and the other was from my sister.

2. Mary _____*forgot*_____ her book this morning, so she sat with me and shared my book.

3. Did you buy tickets for the concert next week? I _____*stood*_____ in line for more than two hours to buy them! It is a very popular concert.

4. I need to improve my pronunciation in English. Sometimes when I speak, people don't _____*understood*_____ me.

5. Where is Ali today? He has never _____*came*_____ to class late. I hope he isn't sick.

6. My best friend just _____*became*_____ an American citizen. He is very happy!

7. Sarah is a great athlete. She has _____*ran*_____ in many races. She is very fast.

8. It is 9:06 P.M. The movie has already _____*began*_____. Let's hurry! We are really late.

BUILDING VOCABULARY SKILLS

A. Vocabulary Review

Match the words in column A with their meanings in column B.

	A		B
e	1. slip	a.	freedom
j	2. artificial	b.	put in order
a	3. independence	c.	not together
f	4. dye	d.	right now
c	5. separate	e.	almost fall
h	6. invent	f.	color
d	7. immediately	g.	nation
i	8. strengthen	h.	make for the first time
b	9. arrange	i.	make stronger
g	10. country	j.	not real

B. Context Clues

Choose the answer that is closest in meaning to the words in bold print. Use context clues.

1. Sir Richard Burton was a great **explorer.** He was the first person to discover Lake Victoria, the source of the Nile River.

   a. inventor

   b. a businessman

   c. a person who looks for new places and information

   d. a person who makes special messages in code

2. Ferdinand Magellan's ship was the first ship to make a **voyage** around the world.

   a. trip   c. race

   b. flight   d. map

3. Some people like to keep a **journal.** They write in it every day. They write about what they did, what happened to them, and what they thought about.

   a. a textbook   c. a magazine about scientific research

   b. a novel   d. a notebook about daily activities

4. Louise studies **geography.** She is learning about mountains, deserts, rivers, and oceans of different places in the world. She also reads about people, plants, animals, and natural resources.

   a. the study of science

   b. the study of people and society

   c. the study of music and art

   d. the study of the land and people of an area

5. My family lives in a **distant** suburb of Tokyo. We have to drive for a long time to reach the center of Tokyo.

   a. near   c. similar

   b. far   d. foreign

6. I looked everywhere for my car keys. Finally I **discovered** them in the bottom of my bookbag!
   a. found
   b. put
   c. covered
   d. lost

7. Farmers raise **cattle** for milk and beef.
   a. pigs
   b. horses
   c. sheep
   d. cows

Unit 9 — Captain Cook

Pre-reading

1. What famous explorers do you know of?
2. How did people make maps of new areas of the world?
3. What do you think life is like for an explorer?

Captain James Cook was a great explorer. He traveled to new and unknown places. Before he began exploring, maps of the Pacific Ocean showed almost nothing. He visited hundreds of islands and put them in the correct places on the map. He made maps of the coastlines of Australia and New Zealand. He

5 also claimed these areas for England—they became English colonies.

On each of his three long voyages, Captain Cook wrote in a journal every day. He wrote about what happened on the ship. When he visited new places, he wrote details about the weather and the geography. He also wrote about the people who lived there, and he described the plants and animals. His journals

10 were full of new information about distant places.

78

James Cook was born in England in 1728. His parents were poor farm workers. James had a very limited education and went to work for a storekeeper when he was still very young. When he was 18 years old he went to work for a ship company. At age 27 he joined the navy and fought in the

15   war against France in Canada. During that time he made maps of the eastern coast of Canada.

In 1768, King George II of England made him the captain of a ship and sent him to the Pacific. He was gone for nearly three years. He explored the coastlines of Australia and New Zealand. He made maps of the Pacific and of

20   the islands. He wrote in his journal about life in these distant places. When he returned to England he was a national hero.

For a long time, Europeans believed that there was a great continent south of the equator. They thought it covered most of what is really the South Pacific Ocean. In 1772, Captain Cook went on his second voyage in the

25   Pacific. He went to find this great southern continent. He tried to sail from New Zealand to the southern tip of South America, but there was too much ice. However, he was the first person to cross the Antarctic Circle, and of course he discovered that there was no great southern continent.

James Cook was a good captain. He always took care of his sailors. He gave

30   them good food to eat on their long voyages so they would not get sick. He was also kind to the island people that he met. He gave them new kinds of plants and animals, such as cattle, sheep, goats, and pigs.

In 1776, Captain Cook started his third voyage. On this trip he became the first European to visit the Hawaiian Islands. He made important maps of the

35   west coast of North America. He crossed the Arctic Circle and met Eskimos.

When he finished mapping the North American coast, he returned to Hawaii. Unfortunately, some of Cook's men and the native people began fighting, and Captain Cook was killed. One of his men, James King, completed Captain Cook's journal of his final voyage.

40   Captain James Cook was one of the greatest explorers in history. His voyages and journals helped people understand the geography of the Pacific and South Pacific Oceans. He discovered that there was no great land area south of South America. He was the first person to cross the Antarctic Circle.

WORKING WITH VOCABULARY

A. Focus on the Reading

Choose the best word for each sentence.

cattle	details	equator	journal
coastlines	discovered	explorer	tip
continent	distant	geography	voyages

1. Captain James Cook was a great _explorer_. He traveled to new and unknown places.

2. On each of his three long voyages, Captain Cook wrote in a _journal_ every day.

3. When he visited new places, he wrote _details_ about the weather and the _geography_.

4. His journals were full of new information about _distant_ places.

5. He explored the _coastlines_ of Australia and New Zealand.

6. For a long time, Europeans believed that there was a great continent south of the _equator_.

7. Captain Cook tried to sail from New Zealand to the southern _tip_ of South America, but there was too much ice.

8. However, he was the first person to cross the Antarctic Circle, and of course he discovered that there was no great southern _continent_.

9. He was also kind to the island people that he met. He gave them new kinds of plants and animals, such as _cattle_, sheep, goats, and pigs.

10. Captain Cook was one of the greatest explorers in history. His _voyages_ and journals helped people understand the geography of the Pacific and South Pacific Oceans.

B. Focus on New Contexts

Choose the best word for each sentence.

cattle	details	equator	journal
coastlines	discovered	explorer	tips
continents	distant	geography	voyages

1. Christopher Columbus was another famous _explorer_. He traveled the oceans and discovered new land.

2. Ecuador, Kenya, and Indonesia are located on the _equator_. It is usually very hot there.

3. My brother studies _geography_ at the university. He loves to learn about new places. He reads about mountains, oceans, plants, and people.

4. Icebergs are huge pieces of ice that float in the Arctic Sea. They are very dangerous because only the _tips_ are above the water. The rest is below the sea.

5. I have relatives who live in Spain. I don't know them at all. They are very _distant_ relatives of my great-grandparents.

6. The United States has two very long _coastlines_. One is along the Atlantic Ocean, and the other stretches for miles along the Pacific.

7. Patricia writes in a _journal_ every day when she goes on vacation. She likes to write down where she went and what she did. It helps her remember later.

8. If you say you are from America, you could be from North America or South America. Both _continents_ are called "America."

continent - big piece of land. 7 continents.

pigeon.

UNDERSTANDING THE READING

A. Comprehension Questions

Answer the questions about the reading.

1. What was Captain Cook's nationality?
2. What part of the world did he explore?
3. What did he write in his journals?
4. When did he start working on ships?
*5. Why did he write in his journal?
*6. Do you think sailors liked to work with Captain Cook? Why?
*7. Why did he take new plants and animals to the island people?

B. Details

Write **T** if the sentence is true, **F** if the sentence is false, and **NI** if there is not enough information in the reading to answer true or false.

T   *1. James Cook worked on ships for nine years before he joined the navy.
F   2. Cook made maps of both the east and west coasts of North America.
T   3. Cook gave the world a lot of geographical information.
F   4. Captain Cook found a great southern continent between New Zealand and South America.
NI 5. Captain Cook sailed along the coast of the Mediterranean Sea.
NI 6. Cook fought in France.
F   7. Cook saw Eskimos, Hawaiians, and people from other islands.
F   8. Captain Cook died in England.

C. Main Idea

Check (✔) the three main ideas of the reading.

✓   1. Captain Cook was a great explorer.
____ 2. His parents were poor farmers.
✓   3. He explored and made maps of large areas of the Pacific.
____ 4. He discovered that there was no great southern continent.

___T___   5. He started his third voyage in 1776.

___T___   6. He mapped some of the coast of eastern Canada.

WRITING

Who was a great explorer from your country? Write a short paragraph about this person. You don't have to know exact dates. Just write some information about where this explorer went. When you finish, exchange paragraphs with another student and read about a new explorer.

WORD STUDY

A. Word Forms: Gerunds

A gerund is a verb + **ing.** It is used as a noun. A gerund can be the subject or the direct object of a sentence. It can also come after some prepositions.

Look at the examples:

> **Learning** English is not easy.
>
> George really enjoys **skiing.**
>
> Eileen is very good at **playing** the guitar.

Spelling Notes:

1. *When a word ends in silent* **e**, *drop the* **e** *before adding* **-ing.**

2. *When a one-syllable word ends with one vowel and one consonant, double the consonant before adding* **-ing.**

Change these words to gerunds. Then choose the best word for each sentence. Remember to follow the spelling rules.

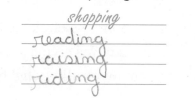

shop	*shopping*	take	*taking*
read	*reading*	map	*mapping*
raise	*raising*	study	*studying*
ride	*riding*	eat	*eating*

1. _____*Studying*_____ English with a friend is fun. You can help each other learn.

2. Do you like _____*readying*_____ the newspaper? I read it every day.

3. Captain Cook is famous for _____*mapping*_____ the Pacific Ocean.

4. I enjoy _____*eating*_____ new kinds of food. I especially like Thai food. It's very spicy!

5. Peter goes bicycle _____*riding*_____ in the mountains every Saturday.

6. I'm tired now. I feel like _____*taking*_____ a nap for an hour before dinner.

7. You can ask the teacher a question in class by _____*raising*_____ your hand.

8. _____*Reading*_____ is a great way to improve your vocabulary. You can read books, magazines, newspapers, or whatever you like.

B. Prefixes

The prefix **re-** means "to do something again."

Here is an example:

re- + write = rewrite (to write again)

First write your composition. Then look at it again, correct the mistakes, change a few ideas, and **rewrite** it. It will be much better after you rewrite it.

Add the prefix re- to each word. Then choose the correct word to complete each sentence.

arrange	read	do	tell	marry	build

1. The students arranged the chairs in the classroom in a circle, but the teacher _____*rearranged*_____ them because she was giving a test.

2. I didn't read the directions, and I did my homework all wrong! Now I have to _____*redo*_____ it.

3. Sofia was married to John. They got a divorce, and a year later she
   remarry .

4. If you don't understand a reading the first time, then you should
   reread it.

5. The hurricane destroyed the old hotel near the sea. Next summer the hotel
   owners are going to _rebuild_ it. The new hotel will be much
   better.

6. Parents often tell and _retell_ the same stories to their
   children. The children love to hear their favorite stories over and over
   again.

BUILDING VOCABULARY SKILLS

A. Vocabulary Review

Match the words in column A with their meanings in column B.

A		B	
d	1. immediately	a.	a flat piece of wood
g	2. over- (prefix)	b.	not natural
i	3. bury	c.	secret writing
e	4. simple	d.	right now
h	5. population	e.	easy
j	6. international	f.	=
b	7. artificial	g.	too much
f	8. equal	h.	number of people
a	9. board	i.	put in the ground
c	10. code	j.	between countries

B. Context Clues

Choose the answer that is closest in meaning to the word in bold print. Use context clues.

1. Judy likes to go bird watching. She sits quietly in the forest and **observes.**
   When she sees a bird, she writes a description in her journal.
   a. looks at things carefully   c. talks quietly
   b. makes a lot of noise   d. draws pictures

2. Look at the **movement** of the trees in the wind! See how the branches bend
   so close to the ground?
   a. color   c. motion
   b. height   d. large plants

3. Some people are fortune-tellers. They say they can **predict** what will
   happen in the future.
   a. forget   c. know something before it happens
   b. change   d. know something after it happens

4. The Sun is a ball of **brilliant** white light. Looking at the Sun directly is
   dangerous.
   a. very bright   c. dark
   b. round   d. circle

5. There are two **paths** through the park. One is for walking, and the other is
   for bicycles. Cars cannot drive on the **paths.** They can only drive on the
   roads.
   a. large highways
   b. sidewalks
   c. narrow places for people and bicycles to travel
   d. open areas where people play sports

6. Alex and his brother are **identical** twins. They were born at the same time on the same day. They look so much like each other that even their parents get confused sometimes!

   a. almost the same   c. brothers

   b. exactly the same   d. similar

7. Seeing stars in the sky above a big city is difficult. Stars are more **visible** in darker places where there isn't a lot of light in the sky. In the country you can see thousands of stars.

   a. hard to see   c. able to be seen

   b. unable to be seen   d. darker

Unit 10

Halley's Comet

Pre-reading

1. What do you see when you look at the sky at night?
2. What do you know about our solar system?
3. Have you ever heard of Halley's Comet? Tell what you know.

When you look at the sky at night, what do you see? You probably see stars, the Moon, and other planets. Have you ever seen a very bright light with a long tail move quickly across the sky and disappear? Maybe you have seen a comet.

5   Comets are bodies that move around in space. They are something like stars or small planets that move around the Sun. Comets are surrounded by gases, and the Sun makes those gases look very bright. Dust can get caught in the gas around the comet and make the comet look like it has a tail.

Halley's Comet is the most famous comet, but we can't see it very often. In
10   fact, it can only be seen from Earth when it moves close to the Sun. This

train = cola de novia

means that this beautiful comet only comes into our sky every 77 years or so. The last time Halley's Comet was visible from Earth was in 1991. Did you see it?

15 Halley's Comet was named after the English astronomer Edmond Halley. An astronomer studies the stars and planets in the solar system. Edmond Halley was born in London, England, in 1656. He studied astronomy at Oxford University. In 1676 he left the university to study the astronomy of the Southern Hemisphere. He wrote a book about the arrangement of the stars in the sky and the movement of the planets. He made the first accurate map of 20 the stars we see in the sky. Halley also observed the Moon and studied how the Moon affects the ocean tides. He helped find a way to measure distances in space. This measurement was used by other scientists to learn about the size of our solar system and the distances of many stars and planets from Earth.

25 Edmond Halley especially liked to study comets. He read about comets and observed them in the sky. He learned about the way they moved around the Sun—each comet follows a different path around the Sun and travels at its own speed. The path and speed of a body as it moves in space is called its orbit. Halley calculated the orbits of comets that he read about or saw himself. 30 He found the orbits for twenty-four comets.

Halley also noticed that the paths of a comet seen in 1531 and of a comet seen in 1607 were identical to the path of a comet he had observed in 1682. He concluded that these three comets were, in fact, the same comet. Halley predicted that the comet would come again in 1758, and it did! This comet 35 was named "Halley's Comet" and can be seen from Earth. The first reports of this comet in history were made in 240 B.C. by Chinese astronomers, so we know that it has been orbiting the Sun for more than 2,000 years. Halley's Comet is not the only comet in our sky, but it is the only one that appears regularly and can be predicted. It is also one of the brightest comets, and 40 people can see it without a telescope.

Like comets, the Earth also travels around the Sun. Sometimes the orbit of the Earth passes through the path of Halley's Comet. When this happens, dust left behind from the comet falls to Earth. The dust burns and makes brilliant lights like falling stars in the sky. You can see this happen every year in May 45 and October. Astronomers predict that Halley's Comet will enter our sky again in 2061. Who do you think will see it?

rovers =

WORKING WITH VOCABULARY

A. Focus on the Reading

Choose the best word or phrase for each sentence.

appears ✓	movement ✓	path ✓	surrounded by ✓
calculate	observed	predicted ✓	tail
identical	orbit ✓	solar system ✓	visible ✓

1. Have you ever seen a bright light with a long ___tail___ move quickly across the sky and disappear? Maybe you have seen a comet!

2. Comets are __surrounded by__ gases, and the Sun makes those gases look very bright.

3. The last time Halley's Comet was __visible__ from Earth was in 1991.

4. Edmond Halley was an astronomer. An astronomer is a person who studies the stars and planets in the __solar system__.

5. Halley wrote a book about the arrangement of the stars in the sky and the __movement__ of the planets.

6. He read about comets and __observed__ them in the sky.

7. Each comet follows a different __path__ and travels at its own speed.

8. The path and speed of a body as it moves in space is called its __orbit__.

9. Halley __predicted__ that the comet would come again in 1758, and it did!

10. Halley's Comet is the only comet that __appears__ regularly and can be predicted.

B. Focus on New Contexts

Choose the best word or phrase for each sentence.

appear	movement	paths	surrounded by
calculate	observe	predict	tail
identical	orbit	solar system	visible

1. Mars and Venus are two planets in our _solar system_.

2. Many people use calculators in mathematics to _calculate_ very large numbers.

3. Some people believe that they can _predict_ events before they happen. Do you believe that it is possible to know the future?

4. Some stars are not very bright. You can only see them when it is very dark. They are not _visible_ in the sky above big cities.

5. An island is a piece of land _surrounded by_ water.

6. Bill and Jack are _identical_ twins. They look exactly the same!

7. Many cities have bicycle _paths_ next to the sidewalks. These are special places for people to ride their bicycles. They are much safer than the street.

8. Clara's new VCR has a special feature. She can play a movie in slow motion if she wants to _observe_ something very carefully.

UNDERSTANDING THE READING

A. Comprehension Questions

Answer the questions about the reading.

1. What are comets?

2. Why do comets look very bright in the sky?

3. Why do comets sometimes look like they have a tail?

4. When is Halley's Comet visible from Earth?

5. What is an astronomer?

6. Name three things that Edmund Halley did or studied.

7. What is the orbit of a comet?

8. When will Halley's Comet appear in our sky again after 1991?

9. When did astronomers first observe Halley's Comet?

10. When can we see the bright dust from Halley's Comet in our sky?

B. Details

Circle the letter of the best answer.

1. Comets move around
   a. the Earth.
   b. the Sun.
   c. every 77 years.
   d. in the Southern Hemisphere.

2. Comets may look like they have a tail because
   a. the Sun is very bright.
   b. gases surround the comet.
   c. dust can get caught in the gas around the comet.
   d. they appear like bright white stars in the sky.

3. Edmond Halley calculated the orbits for
   a. 77 comets.
   b. 24 comets.
   c. 1607.
   d. 1682.

4. In 240 B.C.
   a. Halley was born in London, England.
   b. there were no comets in the sky.
   c. Halley's Comet did not appear in the sky.
   d. Chinese astronomers observed Halley's Comet.

5. Edmond Halley made the first accurate map of
   a. the stars.
   b. England.
   c. the Southern Hemisphere.
   d. the Earth's orbit.

6. The Earth also travels
   a. around Halley's Comet.   c. around the Moon.
   b. around the Sun.   d. every 77 years.

C. Main Ideas

Check (✔) the three main ideas of the reading.

___✔___ 1. Comets are bodies that move around in space.

_____ 2. Dust can get caught in the gases that surround a comet.

___✔___ 3. Edmond Halley's work is very important in astronomy.

_____ 4. Halley's Comet is the only comet that comes regularly and can be predicted.

_____ 5. Chinese astronomers first observed Halley's Comet in 240 B.C.

WRITING

Have you ever thought about traveling in space? What do you think life is like on other planets? Imagine that you are exploring new planets and stars in the solar system. Write a paragraph to describe your trip. Use your imagination!

WORD STUDY

A. Noun Substitutes

In English, we often use a pronoun to replace a noun or noun phrase that has already been used.

Look at this example:

Comets are bodies that move around in space. **They** are something like stars or small planets that move around the Sun.

They = Comets

Read these groups of sentences. Each pronoun is in bold print. Circle the noun or noun phrase that it replaces. The first one is done for you.

1. Dust can get caught in the gas around the comet and make the (comet) look like **it** has a tail.

2. Comets are very beautiful to see. One of the easiest (**ones**) to see is called Halley's Comet.

3. The last time Halley's Comet was visible from Earth was in 1991. Did you see (**it?**)

4. Edmond Halley was born in London, England, in 1656. **He** studied astronomy at Oxford University.

5. The path and speed of a body as **it** moves in space is called its orbit.

6. Halley predicted that the comet would come again in 1758, and **it** did!

B. Suffixes

The suffix **-less** means **"without"** or **"not having something."**

Here is an example:

> Oxygen is an **odorless** and **colorless** gas. ("without odor" and "without color")

Add the suffix **-less** to each word. Then choose the best word for each sentence.

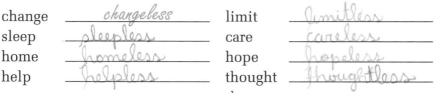

change	*changeless*	limit	*limitless*
sleep	*sleepless*	care	*careless*
home	*homeless*	hope	*hopeless*
help	*helpless*	thought	*thoughtless*

1. The earthquake in Mexico destroyed many large apartment buildings, and thousands of people became _____*homeless*_____. They had no place to live.

2. Aimee told me that she cannot sleep when the weather is so hot. She looks very tired today. I think she must have had a _____*sleepless*_____ night.

3. A baby bird cannot feed or protect itself. It is _____*careless*_____. It needs its mother.

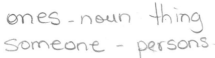

ones - noun thing
someone - persons

4. The list of places in the world that I would like to visit seems
   _____*limitless*_____ ! I will have to live to be a hundred years old in order
   to travel everywhere I would like to go.

5. John made a _____*thoughtless*_____ remark about Anne's speech. He didn't
   realize that he hurt her feelings. He didn't think about how his words
   could upset her.

6. Marie tried and tried to repair her computer, but it was
   _____*hopeless*_____. She will have to buy a new one. Hers cannot be
   repaired.

C. Irregular Verbs

Study the irregular verbs in the list. Then choose the correct verb form to complete
each sentence. Use a verb form from line 1 in sentence 1, and so on.

Present	Past	Past Participle
1. cut	cut	cut
2. hit *golpear*	hit	hit
3. send	sent	sent
4. spend	spent	spent
5. keep	kept	kept
6. feel	felt	felt
7. read	read	read
8. think	thought	thought

1. Evelyn _____*cut*_____ some flowers from the garden and put them
   in a vase in her room.

2. The ceiling is very low in this room. My father is tall and always
   _____*hits*_____ his head when he comes in.

3. Have you received my letter yet? I _____*sent*_____ it more than two
   weeks ago.

4. Anna doesn't ___spend___ much money. She is saving money for a new car.

5. Patty always ___kept___ her money in her purse until it was stolen one day. Now she keeps her money in her pocket.

6. I ___felt___ a little sick last night. I hope I'm not coming down with a cold.

7. Would you like to look at my newspaper? I have already ___read___ it.

8. Did you know that Michelle is from Canada? I ___thought___ she was from France.

BUILDING VOCABULARY SKILLS

A. Vocabulary Review

Match the words in column A with their opposites in column B.

A		B	
_d_	1. native	a.	careless
_e_	2. professional	b.	divide
_f_	3. powerful	c.	unite
_c_	4. separate	d.	foreign
_b_	5. connect	e.	amateur
_a_	6. careful	f.	helpless

B. Context Clues

Tell the meaning of each word in bold print. Use context clues.

1. Smoking **causes** many people to have serious health problems such as lung cancer.

2. Michael always chews on the end of pens and pencils in class. It's a very bad **habit!**

3. You can **prevent** getting a sunburn at the beach by using lotion to protect your skin.

4. The number of students at my school has **decreased** since last year. There are not as many students this year.

5. Laura got very sick last year. She had to stay in the hospital for a week to **recover.** When she returned home, she felt much better.

6. Cigarette smoking has many bad **effects.** If you smoke, you might have trouble with your lungs or your heart. High blood pressure is another bad **effect** of smoking.

No Smoking, Please

Thanks for not smoking

Pre-reading

1. Do many people smoke in your country? Who? (Men, women, teenagers, etc.)
2. What do you know about the effects of smoking?
3. How do people feel about smoking in your country?

Do you smoke? If you do, you are one of more than a billion people in the world today who smoke. If you do not smoke, you are smart, and you are probably healthier than many smokers. Cigarette smoking is common all over the world. It is also very dangerous. Smoking causes many different kinds of
5   serious disease, such as lung cancer and heart disease. People who smoke usually know that the effects of smoking are very bad for them. So why do they smoke?

Smoking is a habit, a bad habit. Many people start to smoke when they are teenagers, usually because they have friends who smoke and they want to be like them. Sometimes young people start smoking just because their parents tell them not to. They want to make their own decisions. But starting to smoke is a very dangerous decision. Once someone starts to smoke, it can be very difficult to stop.

Smoking causes lung cancer, heart disease, and breathing problems. Worldwide, about three million people die every year because of smoking—that's about one death every ten seconds! In fact, smoking is the cause of almost 20 percent of all deaths in the developed countries of the world. Smoking doesn't just hurt the smoker, it hurts other people, too. When a pregnant woman smokes, she is hurting her developing baby. When a man smokes at home, his wife and children are also breathing in smoke and can become sick. Even though most people understand the harmful effects of smoking, they continue to smoke. The number of women and teenagers who smoke is increasing. Cigarette companies make advertisements that interest these groups of people so that they continue to buy cigarettes. Advertisements can be very powerful.

Many people in the world do not smoke and do not like smoking. These nonsmokers are very concerned about the bad effects on people's health from smoking. They have helped pass laws to restrict smoking in public places. Nonsmokers believe that the smoke from other people can also hurt them. This is true. Scientists also believe that "second-hand smoke," the smoke that nonsmokers breathe in from smokers, is very dangerous. Because of this, many restaurants and offices in the United States and Canada limit the places where people can smoke. Many airlines and hotels do not permit smoking at all. Things are changing. People want to stay healthy and live better lives.

It is not easy to quit smoking, but it is the smartest thing to do. If you quit smoking, your chance of getting lung cancer decreases within one year after you stop. After ten years, the chance is almost the same as for nonsmokers. It is possible to quit smoking. If you or a friend or relative smokes, read the advice below. You can start leading a healthier and better life today if you make the decision to stop smoking now. Good luck!

Advice for smokers: If you want to quit smoking, make the decision and do it now. Quitting smoking means changing your lifestyle and your way of

thinking. Instead of smoking and hurting yourself, you can become an active and healthy person. To stop smoking, you need to get plenty of exercise, so your body will relax. Also, drink a lot of water and eat fresh fruits and vegetables to clean your body of the poisons from smoking. You should also
50   try to get a lot of rest so your body can begin to recover from the damage that smoking has done to it. All of these things will make you feel better, and they might save your life.

WORKING WITH VOCABULARY

A. Focus on the Reading

Choose the best word for each sentence.

advertisements	decreases	habit	permit
breathing	disease	harmful	recover
causes	effects	lifestyle	restrict

1. Cigarette smoking is very dangerous. It ___causes___ many different kinds of serious disease, such as lung cancer and heart disease.

2. People who smoke usually know that the ___effects___ of smoking are very bad for them. So why do they smoke?

3. Even though most people understand the ___harmful___ effects of smoking, they continue to smoke.

4. Cigarette companies make ___advertisements___ that interest these groups of people so they continue to buy cigarettes.

5. Nonsmokers have helped pass laws that ___restrict___ smoking in public places.

6. Many airlines and hotels do not ___permit___ smoking at all.

7. If you quit smoking, your chance of getting lung cancer ___decreases___ within one year after you stop.

8. Quitting smoking means changing your ___lifestyle___ and your way of thinking.

B. Focus on New Contexts

Choose the best word for each sentence.

advertisements	decrease	habit	permit
breathe	disease	harmful	recover
causes	effects	lifestyle	restrict

1. I always wonder how fish can ___breathe___ under water!

2. Mimi goes to the health club four times a week and plays soccer on the weekend. She has a very active ___lifestyle___. She is very healthy.

3. Julie's parents don't allow her to drive to school. They don't ___permit___ her to go in friends' cars either. She always takes the bus. Her parents believe it's safer.

4. Shun realized that he was drinking too much coffee. He decided to ___restrict___ the number of cups he drank each day from ten to four.

5. Martha's brother is sick. He has trouble breathing. Her family took him to the seaside this summer to ___recover___. The ocean air is good for him. He will feel better soon.

6. Some people bite their fingernails when they are studying. This is a bad ___habit___.

7. Drinking alcohol can also have bad ___effects___. Large amounts of alcohol can be ___harmful___ to your liver.

8. One good way to avoid heart ___disease___ is never to smoke.
   Keep away

UNDERSTANDING THE READING

A. Comprehension Questions

Answer the questions about the reading.

1. How many people in the world smoke?

2. What kinds of disease does smoking cause?

3. When do many people start smoking?

4. How many people die every year from smoking?

5. What is second-hand smoke?

6. Is it possible to quit smoking? How?

*7. How does becoming a nonsmoker change your lifestyle?

*8. Why is it important to quit smoking now?

B. Details

Write **T** if the sentence is true and **F** if it is false.

_F_   1. Cigarette smoking is common only in modern countries.

_T_   2. People who smoke usually know that it is bad for them.

_F_   3. Teenagers begin to smoke because their parents tell them to.

_T_   4. Smoking is the cause of 20 percent of all deaths in developed countries of the world.

_F_   5. The number of women and teenagers who smoke is decreasing.

_T_   6. Cigarette advertisements can be very powerful.

_F_   7. Second-hand smoke is not dangerous.

_T_   *8. You can quit smoking if you really want to.

_T_   *9. Quitting smoking means changing many of your habits.

_T_   10. Lots of water and fresh fruits and vegetables help to clean the body.

C. Main Ideas

Check (✔) the three main ideas of the reading.

_____   1. Teenagers want to make their own decisions about smoking.

_✓_   2. Smoking causes lung cancer and heart disease.

_____   3. Smoking is not allowed in all hotels and restaurants.

_✓_   4. Smoking is harmful to both smokers and nonsmokers.

_✓_   5. Quitting smoking is difficult, but it can save your life.

_____   6. Smokers know that smoking is bad for them.

WRITING

Advertisements can be very powerful, but they can also be very helpful. Write a magazine advertisement against smoking. Try to make it interesting for young adults. When you finish, show your ad to other students and talk about them.

WORD STUDY

A. Prefixes

The prefix **over-** means "too," "too much," or "too many."

Look at the example:

The world is becoming **overpopulated.** There are too many people. (too populated)

Add the prefix **over-** to each word. Then choose the best word for each sentence.

eat	*overeat*	weight	*overweight*
crowded	*overcrowded*	slept	*overslept*
heated	*overheated*	cooked	*overcooked*

1. I came to school an hour late this morning because I _____ *overslept* _____. I was very tired, and I didn't hear the alarm clock.

2. Jerry had to stop on the side of the road when his car _____ *overheated* _____. He forgot to put water in the radiator to keep the car cool.

3. Anna's grandfather is 93 years old. He said the secret to a long life is never to _____ *overeat* _____. If you don't eat too much food, you will stay very healthy and live longer.

4. I like Mexico but not Mexico City. It is so _____ *overcrowded* _____! I'm not comfortable in big cities with so many people. I prefer the country and the small villages.

5. Mario looks great. He is very healthy and fit. Last year he was a little
   overweight. I think he started an exercise program. Good
   for him!

B. Irregular Verbs

Study the irregular verbs in this list. Then choose the correct verb form to complete
each sentence. Use a verb form from line 1 in sentence 1, and so on.

Present	Past	Past Participle
1. do	did	done
2. say	said	said
3. rise	rose	risen
4. wear	wore	worn
5. teach	taught	taught
6. give	gave	given
7. lie	lay	lain

1. Have you _done_ your homework yet? Let's do it together.
2. The newspaper _said_ that the movie started at 8:00, but it
   actually started at 7:45, so we were a little late.
3. The Sun _rose_ at 6:35 this morning. Did you see it? It was
   beautiful.
4. Charlie _worn_ his new leather jacket on Friday night
   because it was a little cold.
5. Ms. Schulz _taught_ English in Japan for three years. Now
   she teaches in the United States.
6. Paula _gives_ her sister a birthday present every year.
7. Bob _lay_ down on the bed to rest after lunch yesterday.

lie -- resting
lay -- put in down in somewhere.

BUILDING VOCABULARY SKILLS

A. Vocabulary Review

Circle the word that does not belong with the other words. Tell why the other three words go together.

1. chemistry, geography, mathematics, (navy)
2. newspaper, journal, (radio) magazine
3. jeans, denim, rivets, (leather)
4. (advertisement) competitor, inventor, athlete
5. (disease) space, solar system, comet
6. heart disease, (harmless) cancer, sickness

B. Context Clues

Choose the answer that is closest in meaning to each word in bold print. Use context clues.

1. Tea is a very popular **beverage** in China. Coffee is a popular **beverage** in Turkey. Coca-Cola is a popular **beverage** all over the world!

   a. tradition
   b. product
   c. something to eat
   d. something to drink

2. Where do you like to go on vacation? I **prefer** going to warm and sunny places.

   a. want to
   b. don't want to
   c. like
   d. don't like

3. The apples in the cafeteria are not **ripe** yet. They are still green, and they aren't sweet.

   a. red
   b. fresh
   c. ready to eat
   d. ready to cook

4. Look over there! What beautiful flowers! They are so **fragrant,** I can smell them from here.

   a. have a bright color
   b. are pretty to see
   c. have a nice smell
   d. are very dry

5. Have you every seen a cherry tree full of little white **blossoms?** They are quite beautiful.

   a. birds

   b. flowers

   c. leaves

   d. insects

6. I lost my English book last week. I looked for it everywhere in the house. This morning I found it **underneath** my bed! How did it get there?

   a. on

   b. under

   c. inside

   d. next to

Unit 12 · Coffee

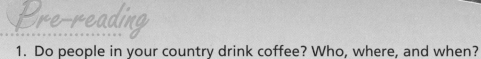

Pre-reading

1. Do people in your country drink coffee? Who, where, and when?
2. Where does coffee come from?
3. Why is coffee popular?

Coffee is one of the most popular beverages in the world. People drink coffee in Africa, Asia, North and South America, Europe, the Middle East, and everywhere in between. Coffee has been a part of people's cultures for thousands of years, and today it is still a favorite drink of millions of people.

5　Do you know the story of coffee and how it came to be so common?

　　There is an old story that says coffee was discovered in Ethiopia a long, long time ago. A man was watching his goats when he saw them eat some small red berries from a tree. After they ate the berries, the goats were lively and active. That night the goats stayed awake late. Because he often felt tired,

10　the man decided to try the berries. He found that he liked the effect, too.

Coffee spread from Africa to Arabia where it was first used as a medicine and a food before it became a beverage. The Arabs kept coffee a secret for many years. Later, coffee spread to Turkey, then Italy, then France. From Europe, the coffee plant was taken to the new world of America. People

15 discovered that the coffee plant grew well in many parts of South America. Large coffee farms, called plantations, were started, and coffee was grown and sent all over the world.

The coffee plant is actually a large shrub, or bush, not really a tree. It can grow very tall (from three to nine meters) if it is left alone in the wild. It has

20 dark green leaves on the outside and lighter green leaves underneath. Small white blossoms appear on the leaves, making the coffee plant look like it's covered with snow. After a few days, the fragrant blossoms fall off the plant, and small berries begin to grow. The berries change from green to dark red in about six months. Underneath the berry skin there is a green bean. When the

25 berries are ripe, they are picked, and the bean inside is removed. This is the bean that produces coffee.

Coffee beans are picked by hand, one by one. Then they are dried and prepared for market. Coffee beans are shipped all over the world. When they reach their destination, different coffee beans are blended together to produce

30 different kinds of coffee. Then the beans are roasted, ground, and packaged in air-tight cans and bags to keep the coffee fresh. Different countries prefer different blends. In Turkey and Arabia dark coffee is preferred. In the United States and Canada the coffee is not so dark. Coffee is also prepared and served differently all over the world. In some places it is made very thick and strong

35 and served in small cups. Other countries serve coffee with more water in it, in bigger cups.

Coffee has become very popular in the United States. Recently, coffee houses or coffee shops have appeared on almost every corner in big cities. These small shops are filled with the smell of fresh-roasted coffee. The tables

40 are full of students, shoppers, and professionals, drinking their favorite kind of coffee. Coffee is now available in flavors such as vanilla and cinnamon, or made with hot milk and chocolate. Foreign coffees are also popular. You can order an *espresso,* a *cappuccino,* or a French roast. You can also order "iced coffee" in the summer. Coffee houses are not restaurants, but they usually

45 offer something to eat, often sweets like cookies and cakes. In the United States and all over the world, alone or with family and friends, a cup of coffee gives everyone a moment of enjoyment.

WORKING WITH VOCABULARY

A. Focus on the Reading

Choose the best word for each sentence.

berries	blossoms	plantations	ripe
beverages	destination	preferred	roasted
blended	fragrant	prepared	underneath

1. Coffee is one of the most popular _beverages_ in the world.

2. Large coffee farms, called _plantations_, were started, and coffee was grown and sent all over the world.

3. The coffee plant has dark green leaves on the outside and lighter green leaves _underneath_.

4. Small white _blossoms_ appear on the leaves, making the coffee plant look like it's covered with snow.

5. The _berries_ change from green to dark red in about six months.

6. When the berries are _ripe_, they are picked, and the bean inside is removed.

7. In Turkey and Arabia dark coffee is _preferred_. In the United States and Canada the coffee is not so dark.

8. Coffee is also _prepared and served_ differently all over the world. In some places it is made very thick and strong and is served in small cups. Other countries serve coffee with more water in it, in bigger cups.

B. Focus on New Contexts

Choose the best word for each sentence.

berries	blossoms	plantations	ripe
beverage	destination ✓	prefer	roasted
blended	fragrant	prepared ✓	underneath

1. Have you ever smelled fresh __roasted__ coffee? When it is still warm from the oven it is so __fragrant__! It smells delicious!

2. In the summer my brothers and I like to pick __berries__ at a farm near our house. We give them to my mother, who makes wonderful desserts with them.

3. In the southern United States there are many old cotton __plantations__. They have large houses and lots of farmland around them.

4. Last night some students from my class ate at Patty's house. She __prepared__ a traditional Thai dinner for us. The food was delicious.

5. Usually bananas turn yellow when they are ready to be eaten. If you buy a green banana, it is probably not __ripe__ yet, and you should wait a few days to eat it.

6. Luisa has a ticket to travel the world. She will leave from New York, fly to Paris, Athens, Moscow, Beijing, and her final __destination__ will be Hong Kong. How exciting!

7. Tea is a more popular __beverage__ than coffee in many Asian countries. In Japan, there is a special ceremony for preparing and serving it.

8. Most kinds of coffee that we buy in the store are not made from one kind of coffee bean only. Many different kinds of coffee beans are __blended__ together for the best flavor.

blended - mix together

UNDERSTANDING THE READING

A. Comprehension Questions

Answer the questions about the reading.

1. Where did coffee first come from?

2. Who discovered it? How?

3. What was coffee used as before it became a beverage?

4. In what part of the new world did coffee plants grow well?

5. What do coffee plants look like?

6. Where do you find the green coffee bean?

7. What happens to coffee after it is picked?

8. What are some of the many different ways to serve coffee?

B. Details

Write **T** if the sentence is true and **F** if the sentence is false. Write **NI** if there is not enough information in the reading to answer true or false.

_F_ 1. The story says that coffee was discovered in Arabia a long time ago.

_F_ 2. A man saw his goat eating the leaves of a coffee plant.

_F_ 3. The blossoms on the coffee are large and red.

_T_ 4. The leaves underneath the plant are dark green.

_T_ 5. The coffee bean is green before it is roasted.

_NI_ 6. People in Europe do not like to drink very dark coffee.

_F_ 7. Coffee is only popular in big cities in the United States.

_NI_ 8. Most Americans prefer to drink foreign coffee.

C. Main Ideas

Check (✔) the two main ideas of the reading.

_____ 1. Coffee beans grow on bushes in Arabia and South America.

✔ 2. Coffee has a very old history as a popular beverage all around the world.

_____ 3. Coffee shops are appearing everywhere in the United States.

✔ 4. Coffee is prepared and served in many different ways.

_____ 5. Coffee blossoms fall to the ground after a few days.

WRITING

Where do you go when you want to be alone to read or to write a letter? Where do you go when you want to meet your friends to drink something and to talk? Choose a place and write a paragraph to describe it. Try to use as much detail as possible.

WORD STUDY

A. Suffixes

Sometimes we can add the suffix **-ly** to an adjective to make an adverb. An adverb describes a verb.

Here is an example:

Sue is a **beautiful** writer. She writes **beautifully. (beautiful + -ly = beautifully)**

Add the suffix **-ly** to each adjective. Then choose the best adverb for each sentence.

Spelling Note: If a word ends in -le, drop the -le and add -ly.

For example: **simple + -ly = simply**

Adjective		Adverb	
careful	_carefully_	silent	_silently_
inexpensive	_inexpensively_	accidental	_accidentally_
easy	_easily_	similar	_similarly_
thoughtless	_thoughtlessly_	possible	_possibly_

1. A student can live ___*inexpensively*___ if she lives in a dormitory instead of an apartment, cooks her own food instead of going out, and rides a bicycle instead of taking taxis.

2. When Monica was helping me wash the dishes, she ___*accidentally*___ broke a glass.

3. Jerry ___*thoughtlessly*___ told Julie about the surprise birthday party we are going to have for her on Friday. I can't imagine why he did that. He was not thinking at all.

4. I had to walk through the house as ___*silently*___ as possible on Saturday night because I came home very late, and I didn't want to wake up my parents.

5. The test can't ___*possibly*___ be on Tuesday! We have to take the TOEFL on Tuesday, too, and everyone will be very nervous. I hope the teacher changes the test to Friday.

6. You will speak English much more ___*easyly*___ in six months. Right now it is difficult for you, but you will improve quickly if you study and practice.

B. Word Forms: Other Words with -ly

The meanings of a few common words with the suffix **-ly** are different from what you might guess.

Look at these words and their meanings.

likely = "probable"

We just finished Unit 11 in our reading book. It is likely that we will have a test on it soon.

greatly = "very much"

Hawaii has changed greatly since Captain Cook visited there in the 1700s.

largely = "mostly"

Blue jeans are popular largely with young people, but older people wear them sometimes, too.

lately = "recently"

Joanna has been absent a lot lately. She missed three days of school last week.

hardly = "not much, only a little, almost none"

Michael hardly ever speaks in class. He is very shy.

(Note: **Hardly** is a negative word. Don't use **no** or **not** with it.)

widely = "in many places, over a large area"

The metric system is widely used in the modern world. The old English system is not.

shortly = "in a short time, very soon"

David should be here shortly. He said he would be back at noon, and it's 11:50 now.

nearly = "almost"

We nearly had an accident last night driving in the rain. The roads were very slippery.

Now choose the best **-ly** word from the list to complete each sentence.

1. I ___hardly___ ever go to the library anymore. I prefer to study at home.

2. Look at the sky! The clouds are so black. It's ___lately___ to rain soon.

3. French and Spanish are two languages that are ___widely___ used outside of France and Spain. Africa and South America are two good examples of where they are spoken.

4. The receptionist said, "I will be with you ___shortly___. Please have a seat."

5. I can't believe it's already the middle of August. Summer is ___nearly___ over.

6. I haven't read the newspaper ___lately___. What's happening in the world?

7. Navajo Indians sell their sand paintings ___*largely*___ because they need the money.

8. Quitting smoking ___*greatly*___ reduces the chance of getting lung cancer.

BUILDING VOCABULARY SKILLS

A. Vocabulary Review

Match the words in column A with their meanings in column B.

A		B	
_e_	1. causes	a.	watch carefully
_f_	2. message	b.	become well again
_h_	3. discover	c.	a small road or way to follow
_g_	4. voyage	d.	all around, on all sides
_c_	5. path	e.	makes something happen
_d_	6. surrounded by	f.	information
_a_	7. observe	g.	a trip or journey someplace
_b_	8. recover	h.	find for the first time
_j_	9. exhibit	i.	limit
_i_	10. restrict	j.	show

B. Context Clues

Tell the meaning of each word in bold print. Use context clues.

1. The Baja **peninsula** of Mexico is surrounded by water on three sides, but it is connected to the mainland of Mexico. It is not an island.

2. Sydney, Australia, has a beautiful **harbor.** Ships from all over the world arrive here. Many beautiful buildings, like the famous Opera House, are also built along the water at the **harbor.**

3. Singapore has a subtropical **climate.** The weather there is very hot for most of the year. During the winter months the temperature is mild, and there is a lot of rain.

4. Marco has an international **trade** business. He buys products from different countries and sells them all over the world. He often travels to interesting places to buy things.

5. My sister and I have an **agreement.** She is quiet when I am studying, and I am quiet when she is working at home. We are both happy with this **agreement.**

Unit 13

Macao

CHINA

TAIWAN

HONG KONG

MACAO

South China Sea

LAOS   VIETNAM

Pre-reading

1. Look on a map to find Macao. Where is it?
2. What is the nationality of the people who live there?
3. What do you think life is like there? What do people do?

Write about your favorite vacation.

Just off the southeast coast of China in the South China Sea are three small islands and a peninsula that connects with the mainland. All together it is not more than 17 square kilometers of land. Even though more than 90 percent of the population is Chinese, this land belongs to Portugal! This little part of the
5   world is called Macao.

The name *Macao* comes from the Chinese *A-Ma-gao,* which means "bay of A-Ma." A-ma was an ancient Chinese goddess who protected people at sea. In the early 1500s, explorers from Portugal discovered the islands, which are just 65 kilometers from Hong Kong. The Portuguese used the territory as a place

10   for trade in Asia. Because of its location in the South China Sea, many
important cities in Asia could easily be reached by boat from Macao. The
Portuguese built two harbors in Macao and traded from them all over the
world. During the next three hundred years, many Portuguese people came to
live there. In 1849, the people of Macao declared themselves free of China.

15   The Chinese government refused at first, but in 1887 Macao became a territory
of Portugal.

Macao today is an interesting blend of Chinese and Portuguese cultures and
modern and traditional life. Street signs and billboards are written in both
languages. The many restaurants offer delicious specialties from both

20   countries or combine them in a very special style found only in Macao. Some
of the buildings along the old stone streets are painted light shades of pink,
blue, and yellow in the old Portuguese style. Other streets are crowded with
modern, high-rise office buildings, hotels, and apartment buildings.
Traditional Chinese markets with fresh and dried fish, tea shops, and stores

25   with beautiful Chinese clothing line the smaller streets. An old church built
in 1602 still sits high on top of the city, reminding people of the Portuguese
history.

On the hilly peninsula of Macao is the city of Macao, a busy center for
trade, tourism, and gambling. Macao is well known for its trade in gold.

30   Millions of dollars worth of gold <u>bricks</u> are imported and sold for currency or
other valuable goods. Tourism is also a very big industry. Tourists come to
Macao from all over Europe and Asia, especially Hong Kong. Both the
peninsula and the islands of Taipa and Coloane offer beautiful and relaxing
resort hotels with private beaches and spectacular views of the sea. There are

35   also many large casinos, or gambling houses, on Macao, where visitors can try
their luck at winning a fortune. Gambling is legal in Macao, and it is a very
big business. The Inner Harbor on the west and the Outer Harbor on the east
are Macao's two ports. They are busy and crowded with trading ships from all
over the world and high-speed boats that bring tourists from Hong Kong and

40   other places.

Fishing is also an important industry in Macao. Because the territory is
surrounded by water, thousands of people go out in boats every day to catch
fish for the markets or the restaurants. Macao's interesting history is visible in
the fishing industry. Small Chinese "junks," or fishing boats, fish next to large

45 commercial boats. The subtropical climate in Macao is also very good for tourism and fishing, with hot and warm weather for six months of the year.

Although Macao is officially a territory of Portugal, it depends on China for most of its food and water. The relationship between Macao and China has always been very friendly. However, when the Chinese gave Macao to Portugal, it was not forever. The two countries made an agreement. By the beginning of the twenty-first century, Macao and its half-million residents will belong to China again.

WORKING WITH VOCABULARY

A. Focus on the Reading

Choose the best word to complete each sentence.

agreement	gambling	officially	territory
billboards	harbors	peninsula	trade
combine	industry	spectacular	valuable

1. Just off the southeast coast of China in the South China Sea are three small islands and a _peninsula_ that connects with the mainland.
2. The Portuguese used this _territory_ as a place for trade in Asia.
3. The Portuguese built two _harbors_ in Macao and traded all over the world.
4. Macao today is an interesting blend of Chinese and Portuguese cultures. The street signs and _billboards_ are written in both languages.
5. Macao is well known for its _trade_ in gold. Millions of dollars worth of gold are imported and sold for currency or other _valuable_ goods.
6. Tourism is also a very big _industry_.
7. Both the peninsula and the islands of Taipa and Coloane offer beautiful and relaxing resort hotels with private beaches and _spectacular_ views of the sea.

8. There are also many large casinos, or ___gambling___ houses, on Macao, where visitors can try their luck at winning a fortune.

9. Although Macao is ___officially___ a territory of Portugal, it depends on China for most of its food and water.

10. The two countries made an ___agreement___. By the beginning of the twenty-first century, Macao will belong to China again.

B. Focus on New Contexts

Choose the best word for each sentence.

agreement	combine	industry	territories
billboards	gambling	peninsula	trade
climate	harbor	spectacular	valuable

1. Times Square in New York City is famous for all of its colorful ___billboards___. They advertise all kinds of products with bright lights or interesting designs.

2. To make lemonade, you must ___combine___ lemon juice, water, and sugar in a glass. Then stir it very well. It's a great summertime beverage.

3. The city of Detroit in the United States is world famous for its car ___industry___.

4. There are not many unexplored ___territories___ left in the world today.

5. Las Vegas is a city well known for ___gambling___. People have won millions of dollars there playing cards and other games.

6. My father has a very ___valuable___ watch. It is made of gold and diamonds. This watch is worth thousands of dollars. He wears it only on special occasions.

7. The Eiffel Tower in Paris offers a ___spectacular___ view of the whole city.

UNDERSTANDING THE READING

A. Comprehension Questions

1. Where is Macao located?
2. What does *Macao* mean?
3. Why did the Portuguese come to live in Macao?
4. In what year did China agree to give Macao to Portugal?
5. What is life like in Macao today?
*6. What is the geography of Macao like?
7. What are the main industries of Macao?
8. What are the names of two of Macao's islands?
9. What will happen by the beginning of the twenty-first century?
*10. How will this change affect life in Macao?

B. Details

Write **T** if the sentence is true and **F** if the sentence is false.

T   1. The name *Macao* means "Bay of A-Ma" in Chinese.

F   2. A-ma was an ancient Portuguese goddess.

F   3. Macao is located in the South Pacific Ocean.

F   4. Gambling is illegal in Macao.

T   5. Tourism and fishing are also big industries in Macao.

_____ 6. The old church in Macao reminds people of its Chinese history.

F   7. Macao is well known for its trade in silver.

_____ *8. Some things will change in Macao after it is returned to China.

C. Main Ideas

Check (✔) the two main ideas of the reading.

_✔_ 1. Over 90 percent of the people in Macao are Chinese.

_____ 2. Macao blends the traditions of China and Portugal.

_✔_ 3. Because of its location, Macao is a busy center for trade, tourism, and fishing.

_____ 4. Macao has many beautiful beaches and resort hotels with spectacular views.

WRITING

Imagine you are on vacation in Macao! Here is a postcard for you to write to your friends at home. Complete the postcard. Then share it with some of the other students in the class.

WORD STUDY

A. Preposition Review

Use your knowledge of prepositions to complete the sentences.

1. Macao became a territory _____*of*_____ Portugal
   _____*in*_____ 1887.

2. _____*In*_____ the city _____*of*_____ Macao, the
   billboards and street signs are written _____*in*_____ both Chinese
   and Portuguese.

3. There are many old Portuguese-style buildings _____*on*_____ the
   streets of this city.

4. Most _____*of*_____ the people in Macao are Chinese. The others
   are Portuguese.

5. There are many beautiful hotels _____*by*_____ the sea.
   Many _____*of*_____ them have spectacular views.

6. _____*At*_____ night, tourists go to the casinos to gamble.

7. High-speed boats bring visitors _____*to*_____ the territory from
   places like Hong Kong.

8. Trade is an important business _____*in*_____ Macao. Gold is
   imported and sold for millions _____*of*_____ dollars or traded for
   other valuable goods.

B. Irregular Verbs

Study the irregular verbs in this list. Then choose the correct form to complete each sentence. Use a verb form from line 1 in sentence 1, and so on.

Present	Past	Past Participle
1. spread	spread	spread
2. grow	grew	grown
3. win	won	won
4. feed	fed	fed
5. bear	bore	born
6. buy	bought	bought
7. steal	stole	stolen

1. Coffee ___spread___ from Europe to the new world of America.
2. People in Arabia have ___grown___ coffee plants for centuries.
3. Which country ___won___ the most gold medals in the last Olympics?
4. My grandfather always went to the park and ___fed___ the pigeons on Sundays.
5. I come from Argentina. Where were you ___born___?
6. Sasha went to the store yesterday and ___bought___ three new CDs.
7. Maggie left her bike unlocked last night, and it was ___stolen___.

C. Suffixes

Many nouns in English end in **-ist**. The suffix **-ist** means "a person who does something."

Look at the example:

   A **novelist** is a person who writes novels.

Complete each sentence with a noun that ends in the suffix **-ist.** The words in bold print are related to the nouns that you should use. Make the nouns plural if necessary. (When you are finished, check your spelling with this list: *chemist, zoologist, artist, finalist, pianist, specialist, scientist.*)

1. Tom really loves animals. In fact, he even works in the city **zoo** on weekends. When he finishes the university, he wants to be a _____zoologist_____.

2. There are many athletes in an Olympic game. However, in the **final** competitions there are only a few competitors. One of these _____finalist_____ will win the gold medal.

3. Michelangelo was a famous _____artist_____. His most famous work of **art** is the painting he did on the ceiling of the Sistine Chapel in Rome.

4. Michiko has studied the **piano** since she was three years old. She practices every day for more than five hours. One day she will be a great _____pianist_____.

5. Roberto is a _____chemist_____ at the hospital. He has a degree in **chemistry,** so he makes medicines in the pharmacy from many different **chemicals.**

6. My brother loves his **science** class at school. When he grows up, he wants to become a famous _____scientist_____!

7. When doctors go to medical school, they can choose one **special** kind of medicine to study. When they finish school they often become _____specialist_____ in one area.

BUILDING VOCABULARY SKILLS

A. Vocabulary Review

Match the words in column A with their meanings in column B.

A	B
f 1. equator	a. allow
e 2. solar system	b. a small fruit
b 3. berry	c. something a person does all the time
g 4. identical	d. the way we live
h 5. visible	e. the planets and stars around the Sun
d 6. lifestyle	f. an imaginary line around the world
a 7. permit	g. the same
c 8. habit	h. able to be seen

B. Context Clues

Choose the answer that is closest in meaning to the words in bold print. Use context clues.

1. Did you hear the weather **forecast** on the radio this evening? I want to know what the weather will be like tomorrow. I'm going on a picnic with some friends.

   a. a man
   b. an announcement
   c. a report about the future
   d. a report about the past

2. Mary's father is in the **military.** He's a captain on a ship. Her brother is also in the **military.** He is a pilot in the air force.

   a. people who work on boats
   b. people who trade goods
   c. a group of people trained to protect a country
   d. a group of people trained to fly planes

3. Did you know that water boils at a lower temperature in high **altitudes?** If you go camping in the mountains, you can see for yourself.

    a. how hot something is   c. how low something is

    b. how cold something is   d. how high something is

4. A movie is actually made of many small **images** that move very fast through a projector. This makes it look like the people are moving, but they are really just photographs.

    a. movies   c. projector

    b. pictures   d. actors

5. If you bring a tape recorder to the lecture at the library tomorrow, you can **record** the information and listen to it again later at home.

    a. play music

    b. make an identical copy of something

    c. listen to music or information

    d. a disc you can play on a stereo

6. Before the astronomer Galileo, people thought that the Sun revolved around the Earth. Now we know that the Earth **revolves** around the Sun.

    a. warms   c. moves behind

    b. moves around   d. travels away from

The earth orbit the sun.

Satellites

1. What is a satellite?
2. What country put the first satellite in space?
3. What do satellites do?

Did you ever wonder how the weather person on the news can know about tomorrow's weather before it happens? How do submarines and ships travel so far out at sea without getting lost? You have probably seen big white satellite dishes on buildings and radio stations. Did you ever wonder where
5   the information that reaches these dishes comes from? The answer to all of these questions is *satellites*.

    In astronomy, satellites are bodies that revolve around a planet. Our Moon is a satellite because it circles the Earth as it orbits the Sun. Comets are also satellites because they travel around planets. But there are other satellites in

10   the solar system that are not natural bodies. They are artificial satellites made by people. Satellites are sent into space for many reasons. Some of them orbit the Earth. Others orbit the Moon or another planet. Some satellites orbit at very high altitudes, as much as 32,000 kilometers (20,000 miles) away from Earth, while other satellites stay close to Earth at an altitude of about 250

15   kilometers (155 miles). Each satellite that people put into space has a special mission, or purpose. There are six major kinds of satellites in space: scientific research, weather, communications, navigation, Earth observation, and military. Each one has its own job to do.

Scientific research satellites travel in space collecting information for

20   scientists. They observe other planets, stars, and the Sun. They record important information that is used to understand the solar system better. Weather satellites also help scientists study changes in the Earth's weather. Weather satellites record images of clouds and storms that are coming. These satellites send weather forecasts back down to Earth. This is how we can

25   know what the weather will be like tomorrow.

Communication satellites orbit the Earth, sending information from one place to another. Stations on Earth send and receive signals, or messages, from satellites. For example, telephone companies use communication satellites to send telephone calls to the other side of the world in seconds. The signal is

30   sent from the Earth to a satellite in space. The satellite receives it, then sends it back down to another station on Earth. Television companies also use satellites to send programs to TVs in houses all around the world.

Navigation satellites help guide ships at sea and airplanes in the sky. The ships and planes receive messages from far away. They also calculate their

35   position at sea or in the sky by the information they receive from satellites. Earth observation satellites are used to observe the Earth's resources, such as rain forests, water supplies, and plants. These satellites are very important. They help us control the spread of disease in crops and forests. They can also detect fires and floods before they spread and become too big.

40   Military satellites include weather, communications, and observation satellites used for military purposes. Some military satellites are called "spy satellites" because they photograph different parts of the world and send pictures back to the ground station. They photograph ships at sea and the movement of the military on the ground.

45   Space satellites are controlled by people and computers on the ground. They stay up in space because they move very, very fast and because the Earth's gravity keeps them there. Imagine tying an object to the end of a long string and spinning it around in the air. The object will remain in motion as long as it is moving fast and the string remains attached. If you stop or cut the

50   string, the object will fall. This is how satellites work. Sometimes they have problems and need to be repaired. This can usually be done from Earth by computers. Other times, people must go up into space to repair them. If they cannot be repaired, they are simply turned off from Earth. Then they are left to float in space forever. This is what is called "space junk."

55   The former Soviet Union was the first country to send a satellite into space. On October 4, 1957, the Soviet satellite *Sputnik 1* went into orbit. *Sputnik 2* went up one month later. This satellite carried a dog named Laika. He was the first animal to go into space. On January 31, 1958, the United States launched its first satellite, *Explorer 1.* Since that time, thousands of satellites have

60   orbited the Earth and other planets in the solar system, collecting valuable information for the people on Earth.

WORKING WITH VOCABULARY

A. Focus on the Reading

Choose the best word to complete each sentence.

altitudes	guide	military	revolve
detect	images	mission	signals
forecasts	launched	record	stations

1. In astronomy, satellites are bodies that _revolve_ around a planet.
2. Some satellites orbit at very high _altitudes_, as much as 32,000 kilometers (20,000 miles) away from Earth, while other satellites stay close to Earth.
3. Each satellite that people put into space has a special _mission_, or purpose.

4. Scientific research satellites ___record___ important information that is used to understand the solar system better.

5. Weather satellites record ___images___ of clouds and storms that are coming.

6. These satellites send weather ___forecasts___ back down to Earth.

7. Stations on Earth send and receive ___signals___, or messages, from satellites.

8. Navigation satellites help ___guide___ ships at sea and airplanes in the sky. The ships and planes receive messages from far away.

9. Earth observation satellites are very important. They help us control the spread of disease in crops and forests. They can also ___detect___ fires and floods before they spread and become too big.

10. On January 31, 1958, the United States ___launched___ its first satellite, *Explorer 1*. Since that time, thousands of satellites have orbited the Earth and other planets in the solar system.

B. Focus on New Contexts

Choose the best word for each sentence.

altitude ✓	guide	military	revolving
detects	images	mission	signals
forecast ✓	launch	record	station

1. Many people follow a tour ___guide___ when they travel to a new city. This person helps them to discover many interesting places.

2. Planes that cross the Atlantic Ocean usually fly at a very high ___altitude___.

3. Many people in the United States have smoke detectors in their homes. An alarm will ring if the machine ___detects___ smoke or a fire in the house.

detect -- find things - to tell something

launched – Push into the air

4. Did you see the ___images___ of the space satellite on TV this morning? It was spectacular!

5. The ___forecast___ for tomorrow predicts rain and cold weather. Remember to wear a coat and bring an umbrella to the game.

6. Most modern office buildings have ___revolving___ doors at the entrance. These doors allow people to move in and out more freely. They also help keep the wind out.

7. Radar is another system that sends ___signals___ to ships and airplanes.

8. I live next door to a radio ___station___. You can easily find my house because of the big antenna on the roof next door!

UNDERSTANDING THE READING

A. Comprehension Questions

Answer the questions about the reading.

1. What are natural satellites? Give an example.
2. What are artificial satellites?
3. What are the major kinds of artificial satellites?
4. What do weather satellites do?
5. How do telephone companies use communications satellites?
6. How do navigation satellites help guide ships at sea?
7. What are "spy satellites"?
8. How do satellites stay in space?
9. What is "space junk"?
10. When was the first satellite sent into orbit?

B. Details

Circle the letter of the best answer.

1. Our Moon is a satellite because
   a. the Earth moves around it.
   b. the Sun moves around it.
   c. it circles the Earth when it orbits the Sun.
   d. it sends information to Earth.

2. Some satellites orbit
   a. the Sun.
   b. the Moon.
   c. Earth and other planets.
   d. (all of the above)

*3. Changes in the Earth's atmosphere are recorded by
   a. communications satellites.
   b. weather satellites.
   c. Earth observation satellites.
   d. weather and scientific research satellites.

4. Satellites stay in space because of
   a. their speed.
   b. the weather.
   c. their speed and gravity.
   d. computers.

5. The first American satellite in space was
   a. Laika, the dog.
   b. *Sputnik 1* in 1957.
   c. *Sputnik 2* in 1957.
   d. *Explorer 1* in 1958.

C. Main Ideas

Check (✔) the main idea of the reading.

_____ 1. Satellites orbit the Earth and other planets.

_✔_ 2. Satellites send and receive important information for many purposes.

_____ 3. The first satellite was launched from the former Soviet Union on October 4, 1957.

_____ 4. Satellites are controlled by people and computers at stations on Earth.

WRITING

Without looking at the reading again, try to remember some of the uses for each major kind of satellite. Complete the chart below with the information. When you are finished, compare your chart with that of another student and see if you can add anything.

TYPE OF SATELLITE	USES
Scientific Research	
Weather	
Communications	
Navigation	
Earth Observation	
Military	

record –
record –

WORD STUDY

A. Word Forms

Notice how these words are related to each other. Choose the best word to complete each sentence. Use a word from line 1 in sentence 1, and so on.

VERB	NOUN	ADJECTIVE
1. decide	decision	(un)decisive
2. organize	organization	(dis)organized
3. distribute	distribution	—
4. prevent	prevention	(un)preventable
5. believe	belief	(un)believable
6. differ	difference	different
7. —	religion	religious
8. harm	harm	harmful, harmless
9. complicate	complication	(un)complicated
10. improve	improvement	improved

1. When you decide to do what is right, you have made the best
   _____ decision _____.

2. Tom's notebook is very _disorganized_. He can never find anything in it.

3. The _distribution_ of food in poor nations is sometimes very difficult.

4. Diseases related to smoking are usually _preventable_. You can prevent them by not smoking and taking care of your health.

5. The story our teacher told us was _unbelievable_! I can't believe it's true.

6. The word *record* has two _different_ meanings. One is a verb and one is a noun.

7. Navajo singers or medicine men are very _religious_ people.

8. Cigarette smoking is very _harmful_ to your health.

    record - makes a copy (v)
    r.

9. Some people think English grammar is very _complicated_.

10. You can really _improve_ your vocabulary by reading all the time.

B. Word Forms: Adjectives

Adjectives have only one form. They can never be plural.

Look at these examples:

Paolo has a vacation for two months.

Paolo has a **two-month** vacation.

It takes six hours to drive from Chicago to Detroit.

It is a **six-hour** drive from Chicago to Detroit.

Change the words in bold print to adjectives with hyphens (-) and rewrite the sentences.

1. It takes **seven hours** to fly from New York to Paris.
   It is a seven-hour flight from New York to Paris.

2. Some universities have a spring vacation for **two weeks.**
   Some universities have a two - week spring vacation.

3. It costs a lot of money to have a telephone conversation for **twenty minutes** overseas.
   It costs a lot of money to have a twenty - minutes telephone conversation to overseas.

4. I would love to take a trip around the world for **six months!**
   I would love

5. We have to take an exam for **three hours** next week at school.
   We have to take a three hour exam next week at school.

C. Noun Substitutes

Read these groups of sentences and study the pronouns in bold print. Circle the noun or noun phrase that each pronoun replaces.

1. (Our Moon) is a satellite because **it** circles the Earth as **it** orbits the Sun.

2. But there are (other satellites) in the solar system that are not natural bodies.
   They are artificial satellites made by people.

3. Scientific research satellites travel in space collecting information for scientists. **They** observe other planets, stars, and the Sun.

4. A signal is sent from Earth to a satellite in space. The satellite receives **it,** then sends **it** back down to another station on Earth.

5. Navigation satellites help guide ships at sea and airplanes in the sky. The ships and planes receive messages from far away. **They** also calculate their position at sea or in the sky by information **they** receive from satellites.

6. Imagine tying an object to the end of a long string and spinning **it** around in the air. The object will remain in motion as long as **it** is moving fast and the string remains attached.

7. On October 4, 1957, the Soviet satellite *Sputnik I* went into orbit. *Sputnik 2* went up one month later. This satellite carried a dog named Laika. **He** was the first animal to go into space.

BUILDING VOCABULARY SKILLS

A. Vocabulary Review

One word in each sentence is incorrect. Find the word and circle it. Above it, write a word that makes the sentence correct. The first one is done for you.

Athletes
1. Artists from all around the world participate in the Olympic Games.

2. Captain Cook made three voyages in the Pacific Ocean. He wrote in his
journal
satellite every day about the details of the weather and the geography of

these new places.

invent
3. Louis Braille blended a system for visually impaired people to read when

he was only fifteen years old.

international
4. English is an artificial language spoken by people all over the world.

5. You can see Navajo sand paintings in ~~stations~~ *museums* and galleries in the

   American Southwest.

6. Milk, cheese, and butter are three examples of ~~denim~~ *dairy* products in the

   supermarket.

7. Navajo artists collect colorful rocks and ~~raise~~ *grind* them into sand for their

   paintings.

B. Context Clues

Tell the meaning of each word in bold print. Use context clues.

1. The United States is a very big country with many different **regions.** For
   example, the southwest is very hot and dry. There are deserts in much of
   this **region.** The northeast coast, however, is very green. This **region** has
   many thick forests and much cooler weather.

2. The Earth's **atmosphere** is observed by scientific research satellites. They
   detect changes in the **atmosphere,** such as high levels of pollution, which
   can affect the weather.

3. In the western calendar, February usually has 28 days, but in leap years it
   has 29 days. This **occurs** every four years.

4. **Carbon dioxide** (CO_2) is a gas that is made of carbon and oxygen. It is
   colorless and odorless.

5. Our teacher always **encourages** us to speak English as much as possible.
   She told us not to worry about making mistakes. She said we should be
   confident and try hard every day.

affect - verb
effect - noun - something influence

The Greenhouse Effect

Pre-reading

1. What is a greenhouse? How does it work?
2. What do you know about the "greenhouse effect"?
3. What changes in the weather have you noticed in your lifetime?

Scientists believe that something very serious is happening to the Earth. It is becoming warmer. Scientists predict that there will be major changes in the climate during the next century. Coastal waters will have higher temperatures. This will have a serious effect on agriculture. Farmers will have trouble
5   producing good crops. In warm regions the weather will be too dry. The amount of water could decrease by 50 percent. This would cause a large decrease in agricultural production.

World temperatures could increase from 1.5 to 5.6 degrees Celsius by the middle of the twenty-first century. And the increase in temperature could be
10 even greater in the Arctic and Antarctic regions. A rise in temperatures could

North Pole   South Pole

139

drought - No rain dry.

cause the great ice sheets to melt, which in turn would raise the level of the oceans by one to two meters. Many coastal cities would be underwater. Why is this happening? Why is the Earth becoming warmer?

15 The Earth and its atmosphere are kept warm by the Sun. The atmosphere lets most of the light from the Sun pass through to warm the Earth. The Earth is warmed by the sunlight and sends heat energy back into the atmosphere. Much of this energy escapes from the Earth's atmosphere. However, some of it remains. Gases such as carbon dioxide, ozone, and water vapor absorb this energy and create more heat. Then this heat is sent back down to Earth, and 20 the Earth becomes warmer.

Recently, however, an increase of carbon dioxide in the atmosphere is causing serious problems. Too much carbon dioxide in the atmosphere prevents heat energy from escaping: Too much heat is sent back down to Earth. And the amount of carbon dioxide in the atmosphere continues to 25 increase. When oil, gas, and coal burn, they create large amounts of carbon dioxide. The destruction of rain forests that absorb carbon dioxide also helps to increase the amount of carbon dioxide in our atmosphere. Some scientists believe that the amount of carbon dioxide in the air will double by the late 2000s.

30 Scientists call this warming of the Earth and its atmosphere the "greenhouse effect." A greenhouse is a special place where plants are grown. It is made of glass or plastic. The sunlight passes through the glass or plastic and warms the air inside. The heat inside escapes very slowly, so the greenhouse remains very warm. This is exactly what is happening on Earth.

35 Another reason why the Earth is growing warmer is because of the amount of ozone in our atmosphere. Ozone is also a gas, a form of oxygen. In the upper atmosphere, very far from the Earth, a layer of ozone helps to protect the Earth from 95 percent of the harmful light that comes from the Sun. If your skin receives too much of this light, you could develop skin cancer. We 40 need the ozone layer to protect ourselves. But the ozone layer is in trouble. Scientists have observed that the ozone layer is becoming thin, and above Antarctica there is a hole. This allows too much of the Sun's dangerous light into our atmosphere and makes the Earth warmer.

Scientists say we must start making changes and planning now. We need to 45 continue to do research so we can predict what will happen in the future. We must burn less coal, oil, and gas. Other scientists believe that the problem is not so serious. They think that the Earth is growing warmer naturally, that we

don't need to worry about it now, and that we should just get ready for life in a warmer climate. Most scientists agree that the causes of the world's climate
50   are very complicated. They say that we must continue to measure the amount of carbon dioxide and ozone in the atmosphere. Scientists also encourage people to learn about the changes that are occurring in the world and how we can all help protect our atmosphere.

WORKING WITH VOCABULARY

A. Focus on the Reading

Choose the best word for each sentence.

absorb	creates	measure	regions
carbon dioxide	encourage	occurring	serious
coastal	escapes	ozone	temperatures

1. Scientists believe that something very _serious_ is happening to the Earth.

2. Farmers will have trouble producing good crops. In warm _regions_, the weather will be too dry.

3. World _temperatures_ could increase from 1.5 to 5.6 degrees Celsius by the middle of the twenty-first century.

4. This could cause the great ice sheets to melt, raising the level of the oceans by one to two meters. Many _coastal_ cities would be underwater.

5. The Earth is warmed by the sunlight and sends heat energy back into the atmosphere. Much of this energy _escapes_ from the Earth's atmosphere.

6. The destruction of rain forests that _absorb_ carbon dioxide also helps increase the amount of carbon dioxide in our atmosphere.

7. Another reason why the Earth is growing warmer is because of the amount of _ozone_ in our atmosphere.

He is interest
the is interested

8. Scientists also ___encourage___ people to learn about the changes
that are ___occuring___ in the world and how we can all help to
protect our atmosphere.

B. Focus on New Contexts

Choose the best word for each sentence.

absorb	create	measure	region
carbon dioxide	encourage	occurs	serious
coastal ✓	escaping	ozone	temperatures ✓

1. Many ___coastal___ cities in Florida, such as Fort Lauderdale and
Miami, are damaged by serious storms every year. Houses and buildings
are often destroyed by the wind and rain.

2. Did you know that the rain forests ___create___ oxygen that we
need to breathe? When they are destroyed, we lose a lot of oxygen in
our air.

3. The east coast is a very beautiful ___region___ of the United
States. There are many small, old towns, thick forests, and lakes with fresh,
clean water.

4. ___Carbon dioxide___ and ___ozone___ are two of the gases in
our atmosphere.

5. Judy is a very ___serious___ student. She always studies and
never misses a day of class.

6. Miles and kilometers are two different systems used to
___measure___ distance.

7. If you live in a cold region, you need to have insulation in your house.
Insulation stops heat from ___escaping___, and it protects your
house from the cold outside.

8. When you spill something on your clothes, you should wash the spot
quickly before your clothes ___absorb___ the liquid and become
stained.

escape- to get out

UNDERSTANDING THE READING

A. Comprehension Questions

Answer the questions about the reading.

1. What is a greenhouse?
2. What causes the greenhouse effect on Earth?
*3. Why do scientists call this the greenhouse effect?
4. What changes will the greenhouse effect make in the world's climate?
5. What gases in the atmosphere cause the Earth to become warmer?
6. What does the ozone layer protect people from?
7. Do all scientists agree about the greenhouse effect?
*8. How can people help protect the Earth and the atmosphere?

B. Details

Write **T** if the sentence is true and **F** if the sentence is false. Write **NI** if there is not enough information in the reading to answer true or false.

_T_ 1. Some scientists say that there will be major changes in the Earth's climate during the next century.

_T_ 2. At the equator, the weather will be very dry, and farmers will have trouble growing crops.

_F_ 3. Some scientists say that there is too much oxygen in the air.

_T_ 4. When wood burns, it creates carbon dioxide.

_F_ 5. The destruction of the rain forests decreases the amount of CO_2 in the atmosphere.

_NI_ 6. Some plastic materials also affect the ozone layer and cause the Earth to become warmer.

_T_ 7. Scientists observed a hole in the ozone layer above Antarctica.

_T_ 8. World temperatures could increase from 1.5 to 5.6 degrees Celsius by the middle of the twenty-first century.

C. Main Ideas

Check (✔) the main idea of the reading.

_____ 1. Some scientists say that there will be a serious greenhouse effect, but other scientists disagree.

_____ 2. The warmer regions of the world will become too dry.

__✓__ 3. Large amounts of carbon dioxide and the hole in the ozone layer are making the world's climate change and become warmer.

_____ 4. Ozone is a gas that help protects us from the Sun.

WRITING

Many people are concerned about protecting the environment. What do people in your country do to help solve problems such as pollution and too much garbage and traffic? What programs does your country have to help keep the environment safe? Do you have any ideas that could help? Write about them, then share your ideas with other students.

WORD STUDY

A. Word Forms: Nouns

Some common noun endings are **-sion, -tion, -ation,** and **-t.** Look at this list of verbs and nouns. Notice how the nouns are related to the verbs.

VERB	NOUN
provide - *give something*	provision
observe	observation
create	creation
prevent	prevention
distribute	distribution
produce	production, product
populate	population
divide	division
inform	information

Choose the best verb or noun from the chart to complete each sentence. Remember to use the correct verb tenses and singular or plural noun forms.

1. Scientists are _____*observing*_____ serious changes in the world's climate.

2. China and India are two countries with very large _____population_____.

3. Trees and plants _____provide_____ oxygen for people and animals to
   create
   breathe.

4. Brazil _____produces_____ much of the coffee that people around the world drink.

5. The _____creation_____ of gases such as carbon dioxide increases the temperature in the atmosphere.

6. Our teacher _____informed_____ us that there will be a test next week on this unit.

7. There was only one piece of pizza left and my sister and I were still hungry, so we _____divided_____ it in half and both of us had a little.

8. The ozone layer protects us from the harmful light of the Sun and helps _____prevent_____ skin cancer.

B. Prepositions: Review

Complete the paragraph with the correct prepositions.

Something very serious is happening (1) ____to____ the Earth. It is becoming warmer. This will have a serious effect (2) ____on____ agriculture. (3) ____In____ warm regions the weather will be very dry. The amount (4) ____of____ water could decrease by 50 percent. This would cause a decrease (5) ____in____ agricultural production. World temperatures could increase from 1.5 (6) ____to____ 5.6 degrees Celsius (7) ____by____ the middle (8) ____of____ the twenty-first century. This could cause the great sheets (9) ____of____ ice in the Arctic and Antarctic regions to melt and raise the level (10) ____of____ the oceans (11) ____by____ one (12) ____to____ two meters. Many coastal cities would be underwater.

C. Irregular Verbs

Study the irregular verbs in the list. Then choose the correct verb form to complete each sentence. Use a verb from line 1 in sentence 1, and so on.

Present	Past	Past Participle
1. stand	stood	stood
2. hear	heard	heard
3. begin	began	begun
4. teach	taught	taught
5. buy	bought	bought
6. tell	told	told
7. spend	spent	spent
8. think	thought	thought
9. feel	felt	felt
10. meet	met	met

1. We _____ *stood* _____ in line for hours to buy tickets to tomorrow's basketball game.

2. Have you ever _____ *heard* _____ traditional Korean music? It's very lovely.

3. Ahmed _____ *began* _____ to study English when he was five years old.

4. My brother _____ *taught* _____ English in Spain for two years. He really liked it there.

5. I _____ *bought* _____ some flowers for my mom for her birthday.

6. Our teacher _____ *told* _____ us an interesting story about her life in England.

7. John never _____ *spends* _____ very much money. He is saving to go on vacation.

8. Have you ever _____ *thought* _____ about what life is like on other planets?

9. Claudia didn't ___*feel*___ well yesterday so she stayed at home.

10. I ___*met*___ a very interesting woman from Africa at school last week.

BUILDING VOCABULARY SKILLS

A. Vocabulary Review

Complete the chart. Choose words from the list that are related and write them under the correct heading.

journal, orbit, berries, launched, habit, blossoms, continent, disease, explorer, beverage, geography, harmful, signals, breathing, communications, roasted

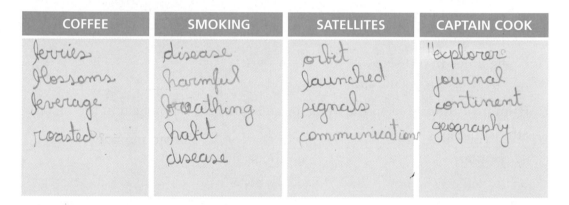

COFFEE	SMOKING	SATELLITES	CAPTAIN COOK
berries	disease	orbit	"explorer
blossoms	harmful	launched	journal
beverage	breathing	signals	continent
roasted	habit	communication	geography
	disease		

B. Context Clues

Choose the answer that is closest in meaning to each word in bold print. Use context clues.

1. Have you ever seen the bones of **prehistoric** animals like dinosaurs in a museum?

   a. living   c. very, very large

   b. dead   (d) very, very old

2. Many people **preserve** fruits and vegetables for the winter. They put the food in jars and cans so it will stay fresh for a long time.
   a. eat
   b. buy
   c. don't like
   (d.) keep in good condition

3. That painting is very **realistic.** The people and animals in it almost look alive.
   a. not real
   (b.) very real
   c. expensive
   d. colorful

4. There are many **caves** in the mountains along the sea in Greece. You can swim inside to look at them. Some are full of beautiful rocks. Others are very dark inside and can be dangerous.
   a. tall mountains
   b. deep water
   (c.) big holes in the side of a mountain
   d. big holes under the sea

5. **Humans** cannot live on the Moon because there is no oxygen in the Moon's atmosphere.
   (a.) people
   b. animals
   c. aliens
   d. plants

claustrophobia — afraid
hydrophobia

Homework.

Unit 16

Cave Paintings

Pre-reading

1. What do you know about life 20,000 years ago?
2. What kind of art did early humans make?
3. Why did people begin to paint pictures?

People have been drawing and painting for thousands of years. No one really knows when painting first began. Archaeologists, scientists who study ancient people and their cultures, have found paintings in different places all over the world. Some of them are close to 30,000 years old! These paintings tell us a
5   lot about people and life in prehistoric times.

The best examples of prehistoric art were discovered in caves in southern France, near the border between France and Spain. In that area there are many mountains made of rock. Inside of these mountains are dark caves. They are very hard to find because the entrances to the caves are often

10   underground or even underwater. The caves are dark and difficult to enter.
There are long, narrow passages around large, sharp rocks that lead into the
caves. At the end of the passages there are large, open spaces. In a place like
this near Avignon, France, a French archaeologist named Jean-Marie Chauvet
found paintings more than 20,000 years old!

15   The walls of Chauvet's cave are filled with paintings. They are perfectly
preserved on the stone of the walls. No sunlight entered this cave after the
paintings were made until Chauvet found them. The pictures cover every
wall. They are images of large and dangerous animals, such as cave bears,
panthers, and woolly rhinos, which no longer exist. The paintings are very

20   realistic. The prehistoric artists used the natural curves and rocks of the cave
walls to make the animals look real. On the floor around the paintings are
animal bones. The bones make the animals on the wall appear even more
alive.

The paintings in Chauvet's cave, like others of their time, were made in

25   three colors: black, red, and yellow. These colors come from natural sources
like charcoal from burned wood, clay, and minerals like iron that are found in
the ground. The artists sometimes used tools such as sticks to paint, and they
sometimes used their hands. Some archaeologists think that prehistoric
painters put the colors into their mouths and blew the paint onto the walls.

30   No one really knows for sure.

Why did prehistoric people make these paintings? What do they mean?
Most scientists believe that the paintings had a special meaning to the people
of those times. Perhaps they painted pictures of the animals that they hunted
for food to bring good luck to the hunters. Perhaps the paintings of animals

35   gave the artists special strengths or powers. Other people think that the
paintings are part of a prehistoric religion. Most scientists agree that the
paintings were very important to the people who painted them. They believe
that the artists made the paintings on stone walls because these artists knew
that they would last for thousands and thousands of years, and they wanted

40   people to see them.

Paintings and other forms of art have been found in different parts of the
world. In Australia, for example, archaeologists have found paintings of
animals on stone. These were made by the Australian Aborigines, the very
ancient people who are natives of the continent of Australia and still live

45   there today. It is difficult to know the age of Aboriginal paintings because they

occur in places that people have returned to many times, each time they have
added more paintings. Scientists have also found examples of prehistoric art
in southern Africa. But, like the Aborigines, people continued to paint in
these places throughout history, so the original paintings became confused
50   with the new ones. Sometimes people have painted on top of the old
paintings.

Scientists agree that the best examples of prehistoric art are the paintings in
the caves of France. These paintings have been preserved in the darkness for
tens of thousands of years, and they will probably remain there for people to
55   see for thousands of years to come.

WORKING WITH VOCABULARY

A. Focus on the Reading

Choose the best word for each sentence.

ancient	caves	hunters	prehistoric
archaeologists	curves	narrow	preserved
border	entrances	passages	realistic

1. Archaeologists, scientists who study ___ancient___ people and
   their cultures, have found paintings in different places all over the world.

2. These paintings tell us a lot about people and life in ___prehistoric___
   times.

3. The best examples of prehistoric art were discovered in caves in southern
   France, near the ___border___ between France and Spain.

4. In that area there are many mountains made of rock. Inside these
   mountains are dark ___caves___ .

5. They are very hard to find because the ___entrances___ to the caves
   are often underground or underwater.

6. The caves are difficult to enter. There are long, ___narrow___
   passages around large, sharp rocks that lead into the cave.

7. At the end of the ___passages___ there are large, open spaces.

extinct - No exists any more

8. The paintings are very ___realistic___. The prehistoric artists used the natural ___curves___ and rocks of the cave walls to make the animals look real.

9. What do these paintings mean? Perhaps they painted pictures of the animals that they hunted for food to bring good luck to the ___hunters___.

10. These paintings have been ___preserved___ in the darkness for tens of thousands of years, and they will probably remain there for people to see for thousands of years to come.

B. Focus on New Contexts

Choose the best word for each sentence.

ancient	caves	hunter	prehistoric
archaeologists	curves	narrow	preserved
border	entrance	passages	realistic

1. The streets in the old section of Rome are very ___narrow___. They were made hundreds of years ago before cars were invented. They are <u>not wide</u> enough for cars, but they are filled with people and motorcycles.

2. Dinosaurs and other ___prehistoric___ animals no longer exist. They died millions of years ago.

3. I will wait for you at the library after school tomorrow so we can study together for the test. Look for me outside by the ___entrance___. I'll be there at 3:15.

4. The bicycle path that goes up the hill is not straight. It is full of ___curves___, so be careful when you are coming down the hill. Don't go too fast.

5. Scientists found a small insect trapped in the liquid from a tree. It is perfectly ___preserved___. They think that this insect is several million years old!

6. You need to show your passport when you cross the ___border___ from one country to another.

7. I know the fighting in movies is not real, but sometimes it looks so ___realistic___ that I can't believe it's not really happening.

8. In some old castles in England there are secret ___passages___ in the basement. People can move from one part of the castle to another without anyone knowing.

UNDERSTANDING THE READING

A. Comprehension Questions

Answer the questions about the reading.

1. How long have people been drawing and painting?
2. What do these prehistoric paintings tell us about?
3. Where were the best examples of prehistoric art discovered?
4. Describe the caves in southern France.
5. Who is Jean-Marie Chauvet?
6. What did Chauvet find?
7. How did the prehistoric artists make the paintings?
*8. What importance did painting have in the life of early humans?
9. Who made the paintings in Australia?
*10. Why are the paintings in southern Africa not the best examples of prehistoric art?

B. Details

Write **T** if the sentence is true and **F** if it is false.

___F___ 1. Archaeologists have found paintings more than 50,000 years old.

___T___ 2. Chauvet's cave is located near Avignon, France.

___F___ 3. The paintings of animals in Chauvet's cave are not very realistic.

___T___ 4. Prehistoric artists usually used only three colors in their paintings.

___F___ 5. Scientists believe that art was not very important to early humans.

_____ 6. The ancient people of southern Africa and Australia never returned to the places where they made paintings.

C. Main Ideas

Check (✔) the two main ideas of the reading.

_____ 1. Prehistoric people painted animals for good luck and strength.

___✓___ 2. The paintings in the caves of France are excellent examples of prehistoric art because they are very old and perfectly preserved.

___✓___ 3. For more than 30,000 years art has been an important part of people's lives.

_____ 4. The cave paintings of Avignon are very realistic.

_____ 5. People in Africa and Australia also painted animals on stone.

WRITING

Imagine that you were the first person to discover the cave paintings near Avignon, France. Write a short journal entry that tells what you saw and how you felt.

WORD STUDY

A. Suffixes

Adjectives that end with the suffix **-ive** mean "able to do something."

Here is an example:

The ozone is a **protective** layer in the Earth's atmosphere. It protects people from the harmful light of the Sun.

Look at the list of adjectives with the suffix **-ive.** Notice how they are related to other words. Then choose the best adjective for each sentence.

ADJECTIVE	OTHER FORMS
protective	protect (verb)
destructive	destruction (noun)
(un)creative	create (verb)
preventive	prevention (noun)
(un)productive	produce (verb)
(un)imaginative	imagine (verb)
(in)active	act (verb)

1. Artists are very _____creative_____ people. They are able to create something interesting or beautiful where there was nothing.

2. I worked at home yesterday and was very _____productive_____. In fact, I think I produce more when I work at home rather than in the office.

3. Hurricanes and other storms can be very _____destructive_____. They can destroy buildings and cars with strong wind and rain.

4. Young children are often very _____active_____. They have a lot of energy and run around and play all day long.

5. Edward tells the most _____imaginative_____ stories! He makes up the most interesting characters and events.
   caracters

B. Irregular Verbs

Study the irregular verbs in this list. Then choose the correct verb form to complete each sentence. Use a verb from line 1 in sentence 1, and so on.

Present	Past	Past Participle
1. blow	blew	blown
2. swim	swam	swum
3. drink	drank	drunk
4. sweep	swept	swept
5. choose	chose	chosen
6. fly	flew	flown

1. The wind _____*blew*_____ very hard last night during the storm.

2. Last summer my friends and I _____*swam*_____ in the sea every day.

3. Have you ever _____*drunk*_____ lemonade? It's very good when you're hot and thirsty.

4. After dinner Mary _____*swept*_____ the kitchen floor and washed the dishes.

5. Have you _____*chosen*_____ a topic for your composition?

6. I have never _____*flown*_____ on the Concorde, but I would really like to someday.

C. Noun Substitutes

Read these groups of sentences and study the pronouns in bold print. Circle the noun or noun phrase that each pronoun replaces.

1. Archaeologists, scientists who study ancient people and their cultures, have found paintings in different places all over the world. Some of **them** are close to 30,000 years old!

2. Inside of the mountains are caves. **They** are very hard to find because the entrances are often underground or underwater.

3. The walls of Chauvet's cave are filled with paintings. **They** are perfectly preserved on the stone of the walls.

4. No sunlight or people entered this cave after the paintings were made until Chauvet found **them.**

5. The pictures cover every wall. **They** are images of large and dangerous animals, such as cave bears, panthers, and woolly rhinos, which no longer exist.

6. Most scientists agree that the paintings were very important to the people who painted them. **They** believe that the artists made the paintings on stone walls because these artists knew that they would last for thousands of years, and **they** wanted people to see them.

BUILDING VOCABULARY SKILLS

A. Vocabulary Review

Match the words in column A with their meanings in column B.

A	B
_d_ 1. attractive	a. work to make money
_h_ 2. connect	b. country
_g_ 3. century	c. put in an order
_e_ 4. town	d. nice to look at
_b_ 5. nation	e. small city
_a_ 6. earn	f. feed and help to grow
_f_ 7. raise	g. one hundred years
_c_ 8. arrange	h. put together

B. Context Clues

Tell the meaning of each word in bold print. Use context clues.

1. Because of the strong winds yesterday, the **waves** in the ocean were very big, and it was difficult to swim.

2. Last week Sarah had a **severe** cold. She had a high temperature and stayed in bed for five days.

3. Be careful when you swim in the ocean. The water has very strong **currents** that can pull you out to sea. You can see water **currents** when you look at the water and see it moving.

4. When Michael was learning how to drive, he accidentally drove the car in **reverse** and went backwards into a tree!

5. You should eat food that has lots of vitamins and **nutrients** if you want to be strong and healthy.

El Niño

Pre-reading

1. What do you know about *El Niño?*
2. What causes drought, hurricanes, and flooding?
3. How does the weather affect our lives?

The world's largest weather system is over the Pacific Ocean. Strong winds blow west from the coast of South America toward Indonesia. These winds pile up warm surface water in the west Pacific, making the sea about half a meter higher at Indonesia than at Ecuador. The sea temperature is also warmer
5   in the west than in the east because the cold water from deep in the Pacific pushes up toward the South American coast. This cold water is full of nutrients, and the fish, birds, and plant life grow strong. Rain falls over the warmer water in the west, and the eastern side of the Pacific stays mostly dry.

   Once every four years or so this normal weather system changes, and
10 something very strange happens. The winds that usually blow from east to

159

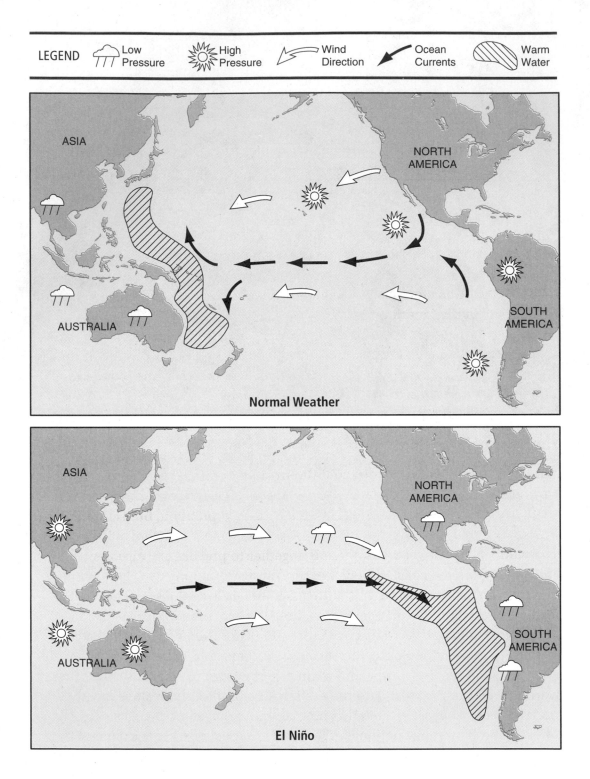

LEGEND 🌧 Low Pressure   ☀ High Pressure   ⇦ Wind Direction   ← Ocean Currents   ▨ Warm Water

ASIA

NORTH AMERICA

AUSTRALIA

SOUTH AMERICA

Normal Weather

ASIA

NORTH AMERICA

AUSTRALIA

SOUTH AMERICA

El Niño

west stop, then blow in the opposite direction. The change in wind direction also causes the ocean currents to reverse. The warm, high water at Indonesia becomes colder and drops to a lower level. The coasts of Ecuador and Peru receive high levels of warm ocean water. This pushes the cold nutrient-rich
15   waters down, and thousands of fish and birds die. Rain follows the warm weather eastward, and terrible rainstorms flood South American coastal countries. At the same time, dry weather and low water cause drought in the western Pacific nations of Indonesia and Australia. The changes in winds and the ocean currents affect weather systems all over the world, and the climate
20   becomes abnormal.

    This strange weather change is called *El Niño.* In Spanish, *El Niño* means "the child" or "the Christ child," since it usually occurs around Christmas. *El Niño* begins in December and continues until March. The changes in weather conditions that it brings are usually mild, but they can be very severe,
25   not only in South America, but in other parts of the world.

    Years ago, in 1982, a terrible *El Niño* occurred. It had a very powerful effect on the world's climate. It caused huge changes in the ocean currents. It caused floods in some areas and <u>droughts</u> in others. There were terrible windstorms and huge ocean waves. These waves swept houses into the sea. *El Niño*
30   caused billions of dollars worth of damage. Thousands of people lost their lives and thousands of others were left homeless.

    In 1983, the winds, ocean currents, and pressure areas started to become normal again. Scientists throughout the world organized research to learn more about *El Niño.* They are now using weather satellites to observe the
35   atmosphere and the ocean. It is a very complicated problem, but scientists are working together to understand the causes of *El Niño.* Then they will be able to predict what will happen and work together to prevent the death and destruction caused by *El Niño* in 1982.

It's not worth it.

	EFFECTS OF THE 1982–1983 *EL NIÑO* WORLDWIDE		
Location	**Phenomenon**	**Victims**	**Damage**
United States:			
• Mountain and Pacific States	Storms	45+ dead	$1.1 billion
• Gulf States	Flooding	50+ dead	$1.1 billion
• Hawaii	Hurricane	1 dead	$230 million
• Northeastern States	Storms	66 dead	—
• Cuba	Flooding	15 dead	$170 million
• Mexico, Central America	Drought	—	$600 million
• Ecuador, Northern Peru	Flooding	600 dead	$650 million
• Southern Peru, Western Bolivia	Drought	—	$240 million
• Southern Brazil, Northern Argentina, Eastern Paraguay	Flooding	170 dead; 600,000 evacuated	$3 billion
• Bolivia	Flooding	50 dead; 26,000 homeless	$300 million
• Tahiti	Hurricane	1 dead	$50 million
• Australia	Drought, fire	71 dead; 8,000 homeless	$2.5 billion
• Indonesia	Drought	340 dead	$500 million
• Philippines	Drought	—	$450 million
• Southern China	Storms	600 dead	$600 million
• Southern India, Sri Lanka	Drought	—	$150 million
• Middle East, chiefly Lebanon	Cold, snow	65 dead	$50 million
• Southern Africa	Drought	Disease, starvation	$1 billion
• Iberian Peninsula, Northern Africa	Drought	—	$200 million
• Western Europe	Flooding	25 dead	$200 million

Source: National Oceanic and Atmospheric Administration
Copyright © 1983 by the New York Times Company. Reprinted by permission.

pile up - make things goes together.
worth of - is kind of value.

WORKING WITH VOCABULARY

A. Focus on the Reading

Choose the best word or phrase for each sentence.

abnormal	damage	pressure	terrible
blow	nutrients	reverse	waves
currents	pile up	severe	worth

1. The world's largest weather system is over the Pacific Ocean. Strong winds ___blow___ west from the coast of South America toward Indonesia.

2. These winds ___pile up___ warm surface water in the west Pacific, making the sea about half a meter higher at Indonesia than at Ecuador.

3. The sea temperature is also warmer in the west than in the east because the cold water from deep in the Pacific pushes up toward the South American coast. This cold water is full of ___nutrients___, and the fish, birds, and plant life grow strong.

4. The change in wind direction also causes the ocean currents to ___reverse___.

5. The changes in winds and ocean currents affect weather systems all over the world, and the climate becomes ___abnormal___.

6. The changes in weather conditions that *El Niño* brings are usually mild, but they can be very ___severe___, not only in South America, but in other parts of the world.

7. *El Niño* caused huge changes in the ocean ___currents___. There were terrible windstorms and huge ocean ___waves___.

8. *El Niño* caused billions of dollars worth of ___damage___. Thousands of people lost their lives, and thousands of others were left homeless.

B. Focus on New Contexts

Choose the best word or phrase for each sentence.

abnormal	damage	pressure	terrible
blow	nutrients	reverse	waves
current	pile up	severe	worth

1. Children need lots of vitamins and _nutrients_ when they are growing.

2. Yesterday someone hit my car while it was parked on the street. There is a little _damage_ to one of the doors. I will have to have it repaired.

3. The Santa Ana winds are strong, hot winds that _blow_ across California.

4. I love to lie on the beach and listen to the sound of the _waves_ hitting the shore.

5. Today is November 2, but the weather is beautiful. The temperature is about 25 degrees Celsius. That's a little _abnormal_ for this time of year.

6. If you don't do your homework every night, it will _pile up_, and then you'll have too much to finish.

7. A _terrible / severe_ rainstorm last night caused the electricity to go out in many parts of the city.

8. Two dollars _worth_ of gasoline is not very much gasoline at all!

Natural disasters

UNDERSTANDING THE READING

A. Comprehension Questions

Answer the questions about the reading.

1. Where is the world's largest weather system?
2. In which direction do the winds normally blow?
3. Where is the water usually warmer, in Indonesia or Ecuador?
4. What is the normal weather like on the western coast of South America?
5. Why is the water near Ecuador good for fish?
6. How often does *El Niño* usually occur?
7. What does *El Niño* mean?
8. What happens to the weather when *El Niño* occurs?
9. What effects did the 1982 *El Niño* have on the world's climate?
10. What kind of research are scientists doing now?

B. Details

Use the information in the chart about *El Niño* to answer the questions.

1. Which country had the most damage (in dollars)? How much was it?
2. What weather condition occured in the Philippines?
3. How many people lost their homes in Australia? Why?
4. What region had snow because of *El Niño?*
5. In which countries were there hurricanes?
6. What did the drought in southern Africa cause?
7. In which country did 340 people lose their lives?
8. What happened in Bolivia?
9. Which regions of the United States had the most damage?
10. Which country had to evacuate 600,000 people? Why?

evacuate - to go out - have to move

C. Main Ideas

Check (✔) the main idea of the reading.

_____ 1. *El Niño* happens around Christmas every four years or so.

___✓___ 2. *El Niño* is caused by changes in the Pacific weather system, and it affects the world's climate.

_____ 3. In normal weather, the winds blow west from Ecuador to Indonesia.

_____ 4. The 1982 *El Niño* caused floods, droughts, and hurricanes.

WRITING

Complete the chart about *El Niño*. Use the information in the reading and in the maps on page 160.

	NORMAL WEATHER CONDITIONS	EL NIÑO WEATHER CONDITIONS
Wind direction:	Blow from east	brow in the epp. D
Ocean currents:	from east	to reverse. D
High level of water:	high level	to lower level
Low level of water:	lower level	to higher level
Cold water:	cold	drop. to a lower level
Warm water:	warm	became colder
Rainy weather:	normal	from flow the warm weather.
Dry weather:		

WORD STUDY

A. Suffixes

You can change some words into verbs by adding the suffix **-ize.** The suffix **-ize** means "to make into (something)" or "to cause to be (something)."

Here is an example:

The clothing company is going to **modernize** its jeans factory.

modern + -ize = to make something (the jeans factory) modern

Spelling Note: When a word ends in y, drop the y before adding -ize.

Add the suffix **-ize** to each word. Then choose the best word for each sentence. Be sure to use the correct tense.

computer   *computerize*   colony   *colonize*
industrial   *industrialize*   special   *specialize*
memory   *memorize*   popular   *popularize*

1. It's best not to try to _____*memorize*_____ lists of words. Instead, you should try to learn how to use new words in sentences.

2. Three countries _____*colonized*_____ parts of the United States and Canada. They were England, France, and Spain.

3. My father is a doctor. He _____*specializes*_____ in sports medicine. He takes care of lots of famous athletes.

4. The Beatles _____*popularized*_____ rock-and-roll music around the world in the 1960s.

5. My school _____*computerized*_____ their registration system. Now when we register for new classes, we just call on the phone, and a computer does all the work. It's very fast and easy.

6. Some countries need to _____*industrialize*_____ in order to compete in the world markets.

Vocabulary.

B. Word Forms

In units 1–16 you studied many common noun endings. Look at the word list below and notice how the nouns are related to the other words.

NOUN	ADJECTIVE	VERB
1. imagination	imaginative	imagine
2. damage	damaged	damage
3. protection	protective	protect
4. measurement	—	measure
5. encouragement	encouraging	encourage
6. discouragement	discouraging	discourage
7. volunteer	voluntary	volunteer
8. region	regional	regionalize
9. provision	—	provide
10. industry	industrial	industrialize

Choose the correct word form to complete each sentence. Some nouns may need to be made plural. Use a word from line 1 in sentence 1, and so on.

1. Come on, tell us a story! You can do it. Just use your
   imagination .

2. Without the ozone layer, the dangerous light from the Sun will
   damage our skin.

3. When you go to the beach, you should _protect_ your skin
   with suntan lotion.

4. What are the _measurament_ of this classroom? It looks very big,
   maybe 25 square meters.

5. My sister always calls me when she needs a little _encouragement_.
   She knows that I always tell her that I am very proud of her and that she
   can do anything.

6. We heard some _discouragement_ news at work yesterday. Fifteen
   people might lose their jobs.

7. Teresa works as a ___volunteer___ at the hospital on weekends. She doesn't earn any money, but she does the work because she really enjoys it.

8. Which ___region___ of the United States have you visited? I have only been to the west coast. I liked it very much. The weather there is wonderful.

9. Most large companies ___provide___ health insurance for their employees.

10. Detroit is a very ___industrial___ city. Most of America's car companies have factories there.

BUILDING VOCABULARY SKILLS

A. Vocabulary Review

Match the words in column A with their opposites in column B.

A	B
_d_ 1. severe	a. new
_e_ 2. abnormal	b. straight
_b_ 3. curved	c. wide
_f_ 4. discourage	d. mild - no bad
_a_ 5. ancient	e. regular
_c_ 6. narrow	f. encourage
_g_ 7. destroy	g. create

B. Context Clues

Circle the answer that is closest in meaning to the word in bold print. Use context clues.

1. How do the winds stop and change direction when *El Niño* begins? No one has found the answer. It is a great **mystery.**

   a. strong wind

   b. severe storm

   c. something we know or understand

   d. something we don't know or understand

2. I think the movie starts at 8:30, but I'm not **definite** about the time. We should call first.

   a. interested   c. certain

   b. going   d. watching

3. Riding to school with Laura every day instead of taking the bus **enables** me to sleep an extra hour before leaving my house in the morning.

   a. allows *to permit*   c. relaxes

   b. makes   d. causes

4. Have you ever **considered** being a comedian? I think you are very funny!

   a. tried   c. studied

   b. thought about   d. practiced

5. The water in the kitchen sink is **dripping** again. It's only a little bit of water, but it's being wasted. We should call the plumber to fix it.

   a. a lot coming out at once

   b. making a noise

   c. a little coming out slowly

   d. not working at all

allow – gave a choose

makes –

causes –

Time

SEPTENTRION

Pre-reading

1. How important is time in your culture?
2. Why do we need time in our lives?
3. What is time?

"What time is it?" "Do you have a minute?" "I don't have enough time."
"Hurry up! We're going to be late!" "Is it time to go yet?"

People talk about time every day. We measure it by the second, minute,
hour, day, week, month, year, decade, and century. But what is time? No one
5   can say exactly what it is. It is one of the greatest mysteries of our lives.

Even though we don't understand exactly what time is, our ability to
measure it is very important. It makes our way of life possible. All members of
a group have to measure time in the same way. For example, we must all
know that it is 9:00 A.M., and stores and offices are open for business. If

10 someone tells you to be someplace at exactly 5:30, you must both know when
that time arrives. Time lets us put things in a definite order. We know that
breakfast comes before lunch. The reading class is after the writing class.
Children can't go out to play until school is over. Time enables us to organize
our lives.

15 The earliest people saw changes around them. They saw day and night, the
changes of the Moon, and the seasons. They started measuring their lives by
these changes. Later, people invented ways to measure and record these
changes. The Chinese invented a water clock in the eleventh century, but the
ancient Egyptians had them long before that. As water dripped from one
20 container to another, it measured the passing of time. People also used the
Sun to divide the day into hours. They made a large dial on the ground. As
the Sun passed over it during the day, the shadow on the dial moved around.
People could tell the time from the position of the shadow on the dial.

Clocks as we know them were probably developed by very religious people
25 in Europe in the thirteenth century. They needed to know the exact time so
they could meet together in church. By the 1700s, people had clocks and
watches that were accurate to the minute. Some clocks were very beautiful.
They had complicated moving parts. Some had figures of people or animals
that moved every hour or quarter hour. Other clocks played music. The
30 movement of the parts is very interesting to see if you open one of these old
clocks.

Today's clocks and watches have quartz crystals inside. They are very
accurate. Watches today can be traditional or digital. Digital watches have no
hands, only numbers that appear on a display. Some watches are very
35 complicated. They keep the time for at least two time zones, they have timers,
alarms, radios, and even very small televisions! Some watches will count your
heart beat while you're jogging, then tell you how far you ran when you
finish.

People in different places think about time differently. In some cultures,
40 time is very important. People make schedules and follow them closely. They
make appointments for a certain time and arrive precisely at that time. In fact,
people might think it is rude to come late. In other cultures, people are more
relaxed about time. They don't consider it rude to come to an appointment
after the scheduled time. These are two different ways of dealing with time.
45 No matter how we look at it, time is still an important part of all of our lives.

In fact - gave more information - expectation.

WORKING WITH VOCABULARY

A. Focus on the Reading

Choose the best word or phrase for each sentence.

accurate	digital	figures	over
consider	dripped	in fact	precisely
definite	enables	mysteries	shadow

1. No one can say exactly what time is. It is one of the greatest
   mysteries of our lives.

2. Time lets us put things in a _definite_ order. We know that
   breakfast comes before lunch. The reading class is after the writing class.

3. Time _enables_ us to organize our lives.

4. The Chinese invented a water clock in the eleventh century, but the
   Egyptians had them long before that. As water _dripped_
   from one container to another, it measured the passing of time.

5. People also used the Sun to divide the day into hours. They made a large
   dial on the ground. As the Sun passed over it during the day, the
   shadow on the dial moved around.

6. By the 1700s, people had clocks and watches that were
   accurate to the minute.

7. Some clocks were very beautiful. They had complicated moving parts.
   Some had _figures_ of people or animals that moved every
   hour or quarter hour.

8. _Digital_ watches have no hands, only numbers that appear
   on a display.

9. People make schedules and follow them closely. They make appointments
   for a certain time and arrive _precisely_ at that time.

10. In some cultures, people are more relaxed about time. They don't
    consider it rude to come to an appointment after the
    scheduled time.

enable —

B. Focus on New Contexts

Choose the best word or phrase for each sentence.

exactly accurate	digital	figures	over *all done*
consider	dripped	in fact	precisely *exactly*
definite	enable	mystery	shadow

1. The train leaves at 7:45. Please meet me in the station at
   ___precisely___ 7:30 so we can buy our tickets and sit together.

2. What happened to the dinosaurs? Why did they disappear? This is
   another great ___mystery___ in the history of our world.

3. Something is wrong with the clock in my car. It's not very
   ___accurate___. By the end of each day it loses almost 15 minutes,
   and I have to reset it.

4. I would love to go to a movie tonight! ___in fact___, there's a
   comedy that I'd really like to see. It's playing downtown. Let's go there.

5. After the football game is ___over___, let's all go out for pizza
   together.

6. Traditionally in the United States, wedding cakes have the
   ___figures___ of a bride and groom on the top of the cake.

7. Do people ___consider___ it impolite to eat in public in your
   culture?

8. ATM and bank cards ___enable___ people to take money from
   their bank accounts from all over the world.

9. There is a little hole in my tent. It rained when I went camping last
   month, and the water ___dripped___ inside all night long. It
   was terrible!

10. Masa's new car has a computerized dashboard. All of the information
    about speed and gas is on a ___digital___ display. There are
    no dials. It's a very nice car.

UNDERSTANDING THE READING

A. Comprehension Questions

Answer the questions about the reading.

1. Why is time a mystery?
2. How do we measure time?
3. Why is our ability to measure time important?
4. How does time enable us to organize our lives?
5. Where was the water clock invented?
6. What are some old clocks like?
*7. What are today's clocks and watches like?
*8. Is it polite or rude to be late?

B. Details

Circle the letter of the best answer.

1. Our ability to measure time
   a. makes us late.
   b. is a mystery.
   c. enables us to organize our lives.
   d. explains what time is.

2. The earliest people measured their lives by
   a. the seasons.   c. the changes of the Moon.
   b. day and night.   d. (all of the above)

3. Modern clocks were probably invented in
   a. China.   c. Europe.
   b. Egypt.   d. South America.

4. By the 1700s, clocks were accurate to the
   a. second.   c. tenth of a second.
   b. minute.   d. hundredth of a second.

5. Some watches today have

    a. alarms.

    b. radios.

    c. small televisions.

    (d.) (all of the above)

C. Main Ideas

Check (✔) the two main ideas of the reading.

___✓___ 1. Measuring time is very important to us, and we measure it several ways.

_____ 2. The earliest people measured time by the changes they saw.

_____ 3. By the 1700s, clocks were accurate to the minute.

___✓___ 4. We don't know exactly what time is, but we need it in our lives.

WRITING

How important is time to you? Complete the questionnaire below. Then compare your information with other students.

Time—A Questionnaire

1. If you have a doctor's appointment for 2:00, what time do you arrive? Why?

   _____

2. You have been invited to a dinner party at a good friend's house. She said that dinner would be at 7:00 P.M. What time do you arrive? Why?

   _____

3. You have a job interview at 9:15 A.M. What time do you arrive? Why?

   _____

4. You own a company. You are going to interview someone for a job. The interview is scheduled for 9:15 A.M. What time do you call the person into your office? Why?

_____

5. Your boss invited you to his house for dinner. He said to come around 8:00 P.M. What time do you arrive? Why?

_____

6. Your best friend asked you to meet him at a coffee shop at 3:30. You arrive at 3:15, order some coffee, and wait. At 4:00 he is still not there. What do you do? How much longer will you wait? At what time do you become angry?

_____

_____

7. Your teacher isn't in class yet, and it's 9:35 A.M. Class begins at 9:00 A.M. What do you do?

_____

8. Some friends from school are having a party. They said it starts at 8:00 P.M. What time do you go to the party? Why?

_____

9. You asked a friend to meet you at a restaurant at 6:00. You're running late. You arrive at 6:30. Is your friend still there? Why or why not?

_____

10. Your mother told you to come home by 10:00 P.M. on a Friday night. What time do you go home?

_____

● WORD STUDY

A. Prepositions

Complete the paragraphs with the correct prepositions.

We talk (1) ___about___ time every day. We measure it (2) ___by___ the second, minute, and hour. Still, it is one (3) ___of___ the greatest mysteries (4) ___In of___ our lives. Even though we don't understand exactly what time is, our ability to measure it is very important. Time makes our way (5) ___of___ life possible. All members (6) ___of___ a group have to measure time in the same way. Time lets us put things (7) ___in___ a definite order.

Is time important (8) ___in___ your life? Do you wake up (9) ___at___ the same time (10) ___in___ the morning every day? What time do you go (11) ___to___ work or school? Do you usually have dinner (12) ___at___ a certain time (13) ___in___ the evening? How long does it take you to drive (14) ___to___ your house each night? All (15) ___of___ these measurements (16) ___of___ time tell us that it is very important (17) ___for to___ all (18) ___of___ us.

B. Noun Substitutes

Read these groups of sentences and study the pronouns in bold print. Circle the noun or noun phrase that each pronoun replaces.

1. But what is (time)? No one can say exactly what **it** is. **It** is one of the greatest mysteries of our lives.

2. The earliest (people) saw changes around **them. They** saw day and night, the changes of the Moon, and the seasons. **They** started measuring their lives by these changes.

3. Clocks as we know them were probably developed by very (religious people) in Europe in the thirteenth century. **They** needed to know the exact time so **they** could meet together in church.

4. Some (watches) are very complicated. **They** keep time for at least two different time zones, they have timers, alarms, radios, and even very small televisions.

5. (People) make (schedules) and follow **them** closely. **They** make appointments for a certain time and arrive precisely at that time.

6. No matter how we look at **it,** (time) is still an important part of our lives.

C. Irregular Verbs

Study the verbs in this list. Then choose the correct verb form to complete each sentence. Use a verb form from line 1 in sentence 1, and so on.

Present	Past	Part Participle
1. bring	brought	brought
2. catch	caught	caught
3. drive	drove	driven
4. fall	fell	fallen
5. hang	hung	hung
6. keep	kept	kept
7. leave	left	left

1. Marie ___*brought*___ a book about France to class last week. It was very interesting.

2. Peter and Louis went fishing last week and ___*caught*___ six big fish.

3. Have you ever ___*driven*___ across Canada? It's a very long and beautiful drive.

4. In many parts of the United States, the leaves on the trees turn red and gold in the fall. Then they ___*fall*___ off the trees and cover the ground. Fall is very colorful.

5. Louisa ___*hung*___ up her coat when she came into the house.

6. Alex ___*keeps*___ his money in a savings account at the bank.

hugs for you.

7. Oh no! I think I _____*left*_____ my house keys in the classroom.
   Let's go back and look.

BUILDING VOCABULARY SKILLS

A. Vocabulary Review

Match the words in column A with their meanings in column B.

A		B
_c_	1. nutrients	a. go backwards
_g_	2. passages	b. takes in
_e_	3. border	c. vitamins the body needs
_h_	4. preserved	d. areas
_d_	5. regions	e. line that divides two countries
_a_	6. reverse	f. very bad
_f_	7. terrible	g. paths or ways through something
_b_	8. absorbs	h. kept very well

B. Context Clues

Tell the meaning of each word in bold print. Use context clues.

1. If you can't find the telephone number you want in the phone book, you
   can call information for **assistance.** *(ayuda)*

2. Many buildings in the United States and Canada have special elevators and
   ramps for **disabled** *(desabilitados)* people in wheelchairs. Remember, not everyone can
   take the stairs.

3. Due to a **lack** *(no enough)* of money and technology, many countries cannot provide
   quality health care to their people. This is a big problem for many people
   around the world.

4. Do you know who to call in case of an **emergency?** *(emergencia)* You should keep the
   numbers of the police, ambulance, and fire department near the phone.

5. After the flooding in South America in 1982, many countries sent food and medical **supplies** to help the people who were injured.

6. It is a law in many countries for children to have **immunizations** before they start school. This protects everyone from disease. Children don't like shots, but they need them to be healthy.

Seizure disorder (apelaisa).
supplies — something you need.
immunization — protection your disease

Pre-reading

1. What do you know about the United Nations?
2. How does the UN help children?
3. What kinds of help do you think children need in the world?

UNICEF means the United Nations Children's Fund. It serves children in communities all over the world. It helps children of all races, nationalities, religions, and political systems in more than 140 developing countries. The purpose of UNICEF is to help provide a better life for children and their mothers. UNICEF gives both long-term assistance and emergency help.

UNICEF was created in 1946 to help bring food and medicine to children who suffered during World War II in Europe. It began as a temporary agency, but became a permanent part of the United Nations in 1953 due to the need for its services around the world. UNICEF's primary concern is to help

10   governments of developing countries improve the quality of life for almost
     one billion children. UNICEF's main office is in the United Nations offices in
     New York City, but it also has more than 40 offices and 100 programs
     worldwide. In 1965, UNICEF won the Nobel Peace Prize for its work helping
     children and building brighter futures.
15   UNICEF works with governments to provide three kinds of services. First,
     UNICEF plans and develops programs in developing countries. These
     programs serve the community by providing health care, information about
     nutrition, basic education, and safe water and sanitation. Then UNICEF trains
     people to work in these programs. UNICEF also provides supplies and
20   equipment that enable the programs to work.
         UNICEF's greatest concern is improving the health of children. It does this
     in several ways. It improves water supplies in undeveloped countries where
     the water is not clean enough to drink. When children drink unclean water,
     they become very sick, and many die. UNICEF works very hard to correct this.
25   It also provides food and teaches people what to feed their children so they
     grow up to be healthy. UNICEF provides immunizations for children to
     prevent serious disease. It gives important vitamins, such as vitamin A, to
     children who could go blind because of a lack of it. It also helps disabled
     children throughout the world.
30   UNICEF helps train teachers and provides equipment and supplies for
     schools. By teaching people to read and write, UNICEF helps people to
     improve their lives. It also helps organize centers for young people and
     women. These are places where people can go for information, education,
     recreation, and support.
35   Most of UNICEF's work is in long-term projects that help people and
     communities grow stronger. But in cases of emergency, such as wars, floods,
     famines, and droughts, UNICEF is fast to respond to people's needs, especially
     the needs of children. UNICEF provides food and medical assistance for
     victims of these kinds of disasters.
40   Three-fourths of UNICEF's money comes from the contributions of
     governments. The other one-fourth comes from the contributions of
     individuals, special events held to collect money for UNICEF, and the sale of
     greeting cards. Every year around the holiday season, UNICEF greeting cards
     appear in stores. They are beautiful cards that celebrate the true spirit of the
45   holidays and the spirit of UNICEF—caring.

chicken pox

WORKING WITH VOCABULARY

A. Focus on the Reading

propose - idea - suggestion

Choose the best word for each sentence.

assistance	disabled	immunizations	purpose
celebrate	emergency	lack *don't have*	supplies
contributions	equipment	nutrition	temporary

1. The ___purpose___ of UNICEF is to help provide a better life for children and their mothers.

2. UNICEF began as a ___temporary___ agency, but became a permanent part of the United Nations in 1953 due to the need for its services around the world.

3. UNICEF plans and develops programs in developing countries. These programs serve the community by providing health care, information about ___nutrition___, basic education, and safe water and sanitation.

4. UNICEF also provides ___supplies___ and equipment that enable these programs to work.

5. UNICEF provides ___immunizations___ for children to prevent serious disease.

6. It gives important vitamins, such as vitamin A, to children who could go blind because of the ___lack___ of it.

7. It also helps ___disabled___ children throughout the world.

8. Most of UNICEF's work is in long-term projects that help people and communities grow stronger. But in cases of ___emergency___, such as wars, floods, and droughts, UNICEF is fast to respond to people's needs, especially the needs of children.

9. Three-fourths of UNICEF's money comes from the ___contributions___ of governments.

lack - not in enough
purpose - reason

contribution - giving something
immunizations - protection for disease.

10. Every year around the holidays, UNICEF greeting cards appear in stores. They are beautiful cards that _celebrate_ the true spirit of the holidays and the spirit of UNICEF—caring.

B. Focus on New Contexts

Choose the best word for each sentence.

assistance ✓	disabled	immunizations	purpose
celebrate	emergency	lack	supplies ✓
contribution ✓	equipment	nutrition ✓	temporary ✓

1. Amy works as a _temporary_ secretary. She goes to different offices for a few weeks at a time when they need extra help. She likes her job a lot because she is always in a new place.

2. You can become very sick from a _lack_ of sleep. Take a nap!

3. Mario works at a store that sells art _supplies_. They have paints, brushes, paper, and pens. It's a great place to shop.

4. I don't think I can finish this work by myself. I need some _assistance_. Can you help me?

5. How do people _celebrate_ birthdays in your country? In the United States, we often have a cake and sing a song to the birthday person.

6. What is the _purpose_ of your trip, business or pleasure?

7. After David took a class about _nutrition_, he developed new eating habits and became very healthy. He said he learned a lot about food from that class.

8. Every year I make a small _contribution_ to UNICEF. I buy their greeting cards to send to my friends during the holidays.

nutrition - healthy food
equipment - what I need or tools.
assistance : needs help
assistants - person. who help

UNDERSTANDING THE READING

A. Comprehension Questions

1. Which children does UNICEF serve?

2. What is the purpose of UNICEF?

3. What are the three kinds of services that UNICEF provides?

4. How does UNICEF improve children's health?

5. What does it do during emergencies?

6. How does UNICEF get the money it needs to help people?

*7. Why should people buy UNICEF greeting cards?

B. Details

Write **T** if the sentence is true and **F** if it is false. Write **NI** if there is not enough information in the reading to answer true or false.

___T___   1. UNICEF is part of the United Nations.

___F___   2. UNICEF is only a temporary agency.

___F___   3. In 1946, UNICEF won the Nobel Peace Prize.

___T___   4. One of the services UNICEF provides is teaching people to read and write.

___NI___   *5. UNICEF helped the victims of *El Niño* in 1982.

___NI___   *6. Adults do not need immunizations.

___T___   7. UNICEF takes contributions from governments and individuals.

C. Main Ideas

Check (✔) the two main ideas of the reading.

_____   1. UNICEF sells beautiful greeting cards to earn money.

___✓___   2. UNICEF provides many kinds of long-term and emergency assistance.

_____   3. UNICEF has programs in more than 100 countries.

___✓___   4. UNICEF's purpose is to provide a better life for children and their mothers.

_____   5. UNICEF trains teachers and provides supplies for schools.

WRITING

UNICEF is a group of letters that stands for several words. UNICEF stands for the words **U**nited **N**ations **I**nternational **C**hildren's **E**mergency **F**und. (This is the original name. It was later changed, and two of the words were removed.) Look up the meanings of the groups of letters in this list in an encyclopedia or dictionary and write the real words for each one. Make a few notes about each one.

1. NATO
2. NAACP
3. GOP
4. NAFTA

5. USPS
6. EU
7. SCUBA

WORD STUDY

A. Prefixes

Sometimes we can add the prefix **en-** to a word to make a verb. The meaning of the new verb is related to the meaning of the original word.

Look at this example:

The ability to measure time **enables** us to organize our lives. It makes us **able** to organize our lives.

Add the prefix **en-** to each word. Then choose the best verb for each sentence. Be sure to use the correct endings and tenses.

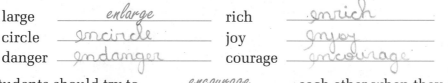

large	_enlarge_	rich	_enrich_
circle	_encircle_	joy	_enjoy_
danger	_endanger_	courage	_encourage_

1. Students should try to _____*encourage*_____ each other when they are learning a new language. Help each other when you can, and practice speaking together as much as possible.
2. If you take this picture to a photo shop, they can ___*enlarge*___ it. Then it will fit perfectly into this frame. You can put it on your desk.
3. We all really ___*enjoy*___ the movie last night. It was a very nice story.

4. Plants need healthy soil to grow. If the soil is not healthy, you can
   ___*enrich*___ it with vitamins and nutrients. Then your plants
   will grow better.
5. Unclean water ___*endangers*___ the health of millions of children in
   the world.

B. Irregular Verbs

Study the irregular verbs in this list. Then choose the correct verb form to complete each sentence. Use a verb from line 1 in sentence 1, and so on.

Present	Past	Past Participle
1. lead	led	led
2. mean *significar*	meant	meant
3. shine *brillar*	shone	shone
4. sit *sentar*	sat	sat
5. ring *sonar*	rang	rung
6. sing *cantar*	sang	sung

1. This road ___*leads*___ directly to the beach. You can't miss it.
2. Your vocabulary really improves if you read a lot, even if you don't
   understand what every word ___*means*___. Keep trying. It really
   works.
3. Yesterday was a perfect day! The sun ___*shone*___, the sky was
   clear, and we didn't have to go to school because it was Sunday!
4. Kung took us to a Thai restaurant last night. We took off our shoes
   and ___*sat*___ on the floor. It was a lot of fun, and the food
   was delicious.
5. Just as I was about to fall asleep, the phone ___*rang*___, and I
   woke up.
6. Have you ever ___*sung*___ in a club with a karaoke machine?
   It's so much fun!

BUILDING VOCABULARY SKILLS

A. Vocabulary Review

Circle the word that does not belong with the other words. Tell why the other three words go together.

1. normal, regular, usual, (abnormal)
2. path, road, (bicycle), passage
3. (disabled,) nutrients, vitamins, nutrition
4. immunization, disease, health care, (education)
5. oxygen, ozone, (coal,) carbon dioxide
6. (assistance,) wars, floods, droughts
7. accurate, exact, precise, (approximate)

B. Context Clues

Tell the meaning of each word in bold print. Use context clues.

1. My family is **originally** from Spain, but we lived in Argentina for almost ten years before we moved to Canada.
2. My grandmother gave me her *receta* **recipe** for chocolate chip cookies. Now I can make them, too.
3. In the fall, I like to **gather** bright-colored leaves. I keep them in a book in my room.
4. We'll have to wait to eat the ice cream. Right now it's frozen **solid.**
5. Did you know that peas grow in a **pod?** Inside the **pod,** the peas sit neatly in a row.
6. It's very hot and **humid** today. There's so much water in the air, it's almost hard to breathe.

1. How much do you like chocolate?
2. What kinds of chocolate foods do you know?
3. Where does chocolate come from?

Lots of people love chocolate. Chocolate milk, chocolate cake, and chocolate-covered cherries are just a few examples of the ways people use chocolate to make sweets and desserts. People eat and drink chocolate all over the world. The word *chocolate* is similar in many languages. Where did chocolate come
5   from originally, and how is it produced?

   Chocolate is native to Central America and Mexico. The cacao, or cocoa, tree was very important to the Maya and Aztec Indians. They used the beans from the tree for currency, or money. They also ground the beans and mixed them with water and vanilla to make a drink. They called this beverage

10   *cacahuatl* and drank it cold. The Spanish explorers noticed that the drink was very popular with the Indians, but they didn't like it when they tried it. The Spanish had sugar, so they sweetened the drink and drank it hot. The Indians named the new Spanish drink *chocolatl,* because it was different from their own beverage. The Spanish took *chocolatl* back to Spain with them.

15   This hot chocolate drink became very popular all over Europe during the next two centuries. People in England opened chocolate houses where friends came to meet, talk, and drink hot chocolate. By 1715, there were 2,000 chocolate houses in London. People really liked chocolate! In the late eighteenth century, French and Dutch companies began experimenting with
20   chocolate. Soon they found it was possible to make it solid. In 1876, a Swiss company produced the first solid milk chocolate bar. It became popular immediately, and soon chocolate was made into many different shapes and sizes and used in many other recipes.

     Chocolate is made from the beans of the cacao tree. This tree can grow only
25   in hot, humid climates. The cacao tree is about seven meters tall and is covered with large leaves. Every year, up to 6,000 small pink or white flowers appear on a tree. Only a few of these flowers produce pods. A pod is about 15 to 20 centimeters long and contains from 20 to 50 beans. A tree produces only about 20 to 40 pods a year. People gather the pods, break them open, and
30   remove the beans. Then the beans are dried, cleaned, roasted, and ground into very small pieces. As the beans are ground, a natural fat in the beans becomes liquid. Chocolate is made from this liquid.

     Milk chocolate is the most popular kind of chocolate in the world. It is used to make most candy bars and other chocolate candy. This kind of chocolate is
35   very sweet. Bitter, or dark, chocolate is also popular. It's not as sweet as milk chocolate. A third kind of chocolate is not very sweet at all. It is sometimes called baker's chocolate, because people use it to cook or bake. When it is used in a recipe with a lot of sugar, such as in a chocolate cake, it is very delicious.

40   Brazil, Ghana, Nigeria, and the Ivory Coast are the world's largest suppliers of chocolate. However, the world's largest consumers of chocolate are the United States and western Europe. The United States also produces a very large quantity of the world's chocolate after it receives the cacao from other countries. The tropical countries that grow cacao consume very little of it.
45   This is probably because chocolate does not keep well in hot weather. It melts!

WORKING WITH VOCABULARY

A. Focus on the Reading

Choose the best word for each sentence.

bitter	delicious	liquid	quantity
consume	gather	originally	recipe
currency	humid	pods	solid

1. Where did chocolate _____ come from, and how is it produced?

2. The cacao, or cocoa, tree was very important to the Maya and Aztec Indians. They used the beans from the tree for _____.

3. Chocolate is made from the beans of the cacao tree. This tree can only grow in hot, _____ climates.

4. Every year, up to 6,000 small pink or white flowers appear on the tree. Only a few of these flowers produce _____.

5. A tree produces only 20 to 40 pods a year. People _____ the pods, break them open, and remove the beans.

6. Then the beans are dried, cleaned, roasted, and ground into very small pieces. As the beans are ground, a natural fat in the beans becomes

   _____.

7. Milk chocolate is the most popular kind of chocolate in the world. It is used to make candy bars and other chocolate candy. It is very sweet. _____, or dark, chocolate is also popular. It's not as sweet as milk chocolate.

8. A third kind of chocolate is not very sweet at all. It is sometimes called baker's chocolate, because people cook or bake with it. When it is used in a _____ with lots of sugar, such as in chocolate cake, it is very delicious.

9. The United States also produces a very large _____ of the world's chocolate after it receives the cacao from other countries.

10. The tropical countries that can grow cacao ————————— very
little of it. This is probably because chocolate does not keep well in hot
weather. It melts!

B. Focus on New Contexts

Choose the best word for each sentence.

bitter	delicious	liquid	quantity
consume	gathered	originally	recipes
currency	humid	pod	solid

1. Water changes from a ————————— to a —————————
when the temperature goes below 0 degrees Celcius.

2. In subtropical countries like Macao, the weather is often hot and
—————————, especially during the winter.

3. When you stir-fry vegetables, you should only use a small
————————— of oil.

4. My sister ————————— some pretty orange flowers from the
garden and put them in a vase in the house.

5. At most airports you can find a ————————— exchange, where
you can buy and sell money from other countries. This is very convenient
when you're traveling.

6. The meeting was ————————— scheduled for 7:30, but it was
changed to an earlier time so that more people could come. Now it's
scheduled for 6:00.

7. In the food section of the Sunday newspaper, there are often several
————————— that you can try at home. I used a few of them and
made delicious meals!

8. People in the United States ————————— more chocolate than
anybody else in the world.

UNDERSTANDING THE READING

A. Comprehension Questions

Answer the questions about the reading.

1. Chocolate is native to what part of the world?
2. How did the Aztec and Maya Indians use cacao beans?
3. How does cacao grow?
4. How is chocolate produced?
5. What are three kinds of chocolate?
6. Where is cacao grown today?
7. Where are the largest consumers of chocolate in the world?

*8. What other foods did the Spanish bring to Europe?

*9. What kind of chocolate do you think Americans eat most?

*10. What are some things you can make with baker's chocolate?

B. Details

Write **T** if the sentence is true and **F** if it is false.

_____ 1. Chocolate originated in South America.

_____ 2. The cacao tree was very important to the Maya and Aztec Indians.

_____ 3. *Cacahuatl* was a hot beverage made by the Indians.

_____ 4. The Spanish liked the Indian drink immediately.

_____ 5. Hot chocolate became very popular in England.

_____ 6. There were 2,000 chocolate houses in France and Switzerland.

_____ 7. Americans made the first milk chocolate bar in 1876.

_____ 8. The cacao tree produces bright pink berries.

_____ 9. Cacao pods contain about 6,000 beans.

_____ 10. Milk chocolate is used to make most candy bars.

C. Main Ideas

Check (✔) the two main ideas of the reading.

_____ 1. Chocolate is used in many sweets and desserts all over the world.

_____ 2. Chocolate was originally an Indian beverage that the Spanish brought to Europe.

_____ 3. A Swiss company produced the first solid chocolate bar.

_____ 4. Chocolate is made from cacao beans that grow in pods on trees in hot, humid climates.

_____ 5. Brazil, Ghana, Nigeria, and the Ivory Coast are the world's largest suppliers of chocolate.

WRITING

You have now read about two similar plants: coffee and cacao. Complete the chart below. Then compare your answers with other students.

	COFFEE	CACAO
1. Where were the plants discovered first?		
2. Where are the plants grown today?		
3. What does the plant look like?		
4. What kind of flowers does it have?		
5. Where are the beans found?		
6. What happens to the beans after they are picked?		
7. What products are made from this bean?		

WORD STUDY

A. Suffixes

Many nouns in English end in the suffix **-age.**

Look at the example:

The Baums have been married for a long time. Their **marriage** has lasted forty years.

Add the suffix -age to each word. Then choose the best noun for each sentence.

Spelling Notes:

1. If a word ends in y, change the y to i before adding -age.

2. If a word ends in e, drop the e before adding -age.

marry	*marriage*	out	_____
post	_____	short	_____
pack	_____	store	_____

1. My friend John likes to collect _____*postage*_____ stamps. He has stamps from all over the world. Some of them are very unusual.

2. Is there a _____ room in this apartment building? I need a place to put my bicycle during the winter when I can't ride it.

3. People in many countries around the world suffer from a food _____. There isn't enough food to feed all of the people. Agencies like UNICEF try to help.

4. Because of the big power _____ at school, all of the classes after lunch were canceled for today. Tomorrow the power will probably be on again.

5. My roommate received a big _____ in the mail this morning. It's a big box wrapped in beautiful paper. I can't wait until she comes home to open it!

6. Takashi's grandparents have had a long and happy _____. They were married 65 years ago.

B. Prepositions

Complete the paragraphs with the correct prepositions.

Lots (1) ___of___ people love chocolate. Chocolate milk, chocolate cake, and chocolate-covered cherries are just a few examples (2) ___of___ the ways people use chocolate to make sweets and desserts. Chocolate is native (3) ___to___ Central America and Mexico. The cacao bean was very important (4) ___to___ the Maya and Aztec Indians. They used the beans (5) ___of___ the tree (6) ___for___ currency, or money. They also ground them and mixed them (7) ___with___ water and vanilla to make a drink. The Spanish added sugar (8) ___to___ this drink and took it back (9) ___to___ Spain with them.

Chocolate is made (10) ___from___ the beans (11) ___from___ the cacao tree. This tree only grows (12) ___in___ hot, humid climates. Every year, pink and white flowers appear (13) ___on___ the tree. Only a few (14) ___of___ these flowers will produce pods. A pod contains (15) ___from___ 20 (16) ___to___ 50 beans. After they are dried and roasted, the beans are ground, and a natural fat (17) ___of___ the beans becomes liquid. Chocolate is made (18) ___from___ this liquid.

C. Word Forms

Study the words in the list. Notice how they are related to each other. Then choose the best word to complete each sentence. Use a word from line 1 in sentence 1, and so on.

VERB	NOUN	ADJECTIVE
1. —	science, scientist	(un)scientific
2. decide	decision	(in)decisive
3. discuss	discussion	—
4. please	pleasure	(un)pleasant
5. consider	consideration	(in)considerate
6. immunize	immunization	—
7. assist	assistance	—
8. sweeten	sweetener	sweet
9. mix	mixture	—
10. originate	origin	original
11. attract	attraction	(un)attractive
12. (dis)appear	(dis)appearance	—

1. Some satellites that orbit the earth are used for _____*scientific*_____ research.

2. I can't _____ which math class to take this year. What are you taking?

3. The Great Books literature club meets every Thursday for group _____.

4. Let's take a drive along the sea today. That's a _____ way to spend the day.

5. Before you make a decision, you should _____ all your choices carefully.

6. Children need _____ to prevent disease.

7. If you need to find something in the library, ask the librarian to
   _____ you.

8. Milk chocolate is very _____. It is used to make candy
   bars.

9. The Indian beverage *cacahuatl* is a _____ of chocolate,
   vanilla, and water.

10. Coffee _____ in Ethiopia. From there it spread
    throughout the world.

11. You can _____ more bees with a spoonful of honey than
    with a bottle of vinegar!

12. I always lose my car keys! I put them here a minute ago and now
    they've _____.

BUILDING VOCABULARY SKILLS

A. Vocabulary Review

Match the words in column A with their opposites in column B.

A		B	
____	1. disconnect	a.	wonderful
____	2. terrible	b.	indefinite
____	3. accurate	c.	sweet
____	4. health	d.	huge
____	5. contribute	e.	sickness
____	6. bitter	f.	incorrect
____	7. liquid	g.	take
____	8. definite	h.	connect
____	9. damage	i.	solid
____	10. tiny	j.	fix

B. Context Clues

Choose the answer that is closest in meaning to each word in bold print. Use context clues.

1. It is a tradition for children to **decorate** eggs with bright colors for the Christian holiday of Easter. They paint the eggs, then place them in a basket on a table.
   - a. cook
   - b. buy
   - c. make beautiful
   - d. break

2. Vincent has a special watch for scuba diving. It is completely **waterproof,** so he can wear it underwater. He also wears it to school, because it is a very accurate watch.
   - a. made of water
   - b. can't be used in water
   - c. can be used in water
   - d. needs water to work

3. Ancient Chinese artists used to make beautiful things, such as vases, plates, teacups, and figures of people and animals, from **porcelain.**
   - a. a material used to make tea
   - b. a material made from wood
   - c. a material used for making dishes and other objects
   - d. a material used for making things for animals

4. Many things are made of **clay,** such as floor tiles, flower pots, and bricks.
   - a. a kind of liquid
   - b. a kind of stone
   - c. a kind of white sand found on beaches
   - d. a kind of rich, red soil from the earth

5. A washing machine **spins** the clothes inside to remove the water when it has finished washing.
   - a. moves in a circle
   - b. moves back and forth
   - c. dries with heat
   - d. washes with soap

Pottery Making

Pre-reading

1. What is pottery? Do you have any?
2. How do people make plates and bowls?
3. What is clay?

Pottery is the name given to a variety of useful or artistic objects made from clay. Pottery can be plates or pitchers, bowls or baskets. Pottery can be large or small, fancy or plain. Pottery is part of the larger family of ceramics. Ceramics are synthetic materials that are not metal or plastic. For example, bricks and
5   tiles are both ceramics. The word *ceramics* comes from the Greek word *keramos,* which means "potter's clay."

Pottery developed in many places around the world at many different times in history. Styles from one region or one time often influenced another. Pottery making began about 7,000 years ago in Egypt and the Middle East. The

10 earliest forms of pottery were objects for use in the house, such as large vases for holding water and oil. Around 3000 B.C., the Egyptians became the first people to decorate their pottery with colors and designs. Similar styles began to spread throughout the Mediterranean region. By 1600 B.C., the people of the Greek island of Crete were producing their own pottery decorated with
15 beautiful designs and images of animals. These designs survived thousands of years and can still be seen in examples of ancient Greek art.

China also has a long history of pottery making. The pottery makers of China were the first to learn to make porcelain. Porcelain is the finest, most fragile type of pottery. It is made from a special, white clay. If you hold a piece
20 of porcelain in the air, light will shine through it. Chinese potters have made some of the most beautiful pottery in history. They exported their work to other countries in Asia and Europe, and soon these countries began to produce pottery influenced by the lovely Chinese art. Today, France and England also produce some of the world's finest porcelain.

25 How is pottery made? First, a potter takes some clay. Clay is a soft, red material from the earth. It looks a little like red dirt, but it's very different. Clay is thick and rich. Wet clay can be worked into any shape. When the clay dries, it will keep that shape. The potter takes some clay and pushes and squeezes it until it is soft and smooth. After that, the clay can be shaped into
30 anything. There are several ways to shape clay. Sometimes potters use their hands. Sometimes they use a special wheel. They place the clay in the center of a round, flat wheel. The wheel spins very fast, and the potter shapes the clay.

After the potter has shaped the clay, it can be decorated. Potters use glaze,
35 which is a kind of paint, to decorate their work. Some glazes are very simple. Other glazes have beautiful colors and designs. The glaze is not just beautiful. It is also useful. The glaze makes the pottery smooth and waterproof. Potters also scratch the surface of the soft clay to make decorative lines and designs. After it is decorated, the clay must be baked, or fired, in a special oven.
40 Baking the clay at very high temperatures makes it hard and strong. Firing also makes the glaze stick to the pottery. When the firing is over, the potter carefully removes the pottery from the oven and lets it cool slowly. If it cools too quickly, it could crack and break.

Since pottery is waterproof, it is very popular for dishes. You can find
45 examples of pottery in almost any home. But pottery can also be found in museums. Some pieces of pottery are valuable and beautiful pieces of art.

WORKING WITH VOCABULARY

A. Focus on the Reading

Choose the best word for each sentence.

ceramics	decorate	influenced	spin
clay	fragile	porcelain	vases
crack	glaze	pottery	waterproof

1. _____ is the name given to a variety of useful or artistic objects made from clay.

2. Pottery is part of the larger family of _____.

3. Pottery developed in many places around the world at many different times in history. Styles from one region or time often _____ another.

4. The earliest forms of pottery were objects for use in the house, such as large _____ for holding water and oil.

5. Around 3000 B.C., the Egyptians became the first people to _____ their pottery with colors and designs.

6. The pottery makers of China were the first to learn to make _____. It is the finest, most _____ type of pottery.

7. How is pottery made? First, a potter takes some _____. It is a soft, red material from the earth. It looks a little like red dirt, but it's very different.

8. After the potter has shaped the clay, it can be decorated. Potters use _____, which is a kind of paint, to decorate their work.

9. Glaze is not just beautiful, it is also useful. Glaze makes the pottery smooth and _____.

10. When the firing is over, the potter carefully removes the pottery from the oven and lets it cool slowly. If it cools too quickly, it could _____ and break.

B. Focus on New Contexts

Choose the best word for each sentence.

ceramics	decorate	influenced	spins
clay	fragile	porcelain	vase
crack	glaze	pottery	waterproof

1. George has a watch that he can wear in the ocean. It's a special watch for scuba diving, so it's completely _____.

2. What beautiful flowers! I'll put them in the _____ on the dining room table.

3. College students in the United States often _____ their dormitory rooms with posters of their favorite musicians and pictures from home.

4. Be careful with that box! It says "_____" on the side. I think it might have glass or something that could break inside.

5. The roof on my apartment building is very old. There's a small _____ in my ceiling, and the rain comes in and drips on me sometimes. We need to have it repaired.

6. Marie is from Sèvres, France. Her city is famous for the _____ they make. It is the most beautiful and expensive kind of pottery.

7. The porcelain of China really _____ the pottery making in the rest of the world.

8. When a CD is inside the CD player, it _____ very quickly while a laser reads the music.

UNDERSTANDING THE READING

A. Comprehension Questions

Answer the questions about the reading.

1. What is pottery?

2. What are ceramics?

3. Where did pottery develop?

4. What are Chinese potters famous for?

5. What is clay?

6. How does a potter shape the clay?

7. What does glaze do to pottery?

8. What is firing?

9. What does firing do?

10. What happens if pottery cools too quickly?

B. Details

Write **T** if the sentence is true and **F** if it is false.

_____ 1. Plates, pitchers, and bowls are examples of pottery.

_____ 2. The word *ceramics* comes from the Greek word for "potter's clay."

_____ 3. The earliest forms of pottery were made in Crete about 7,000 years ago.

_____ 4. Porcelain is made from hard, red clay.

_____ 5. There is only one way to shape clay.

_____ 6. Glazes can make pottery waterproof.

_____ 7. Firing makes the glaze stick to the pottery.

_____ 8. Some examples of pottery can be seen in museums.

C. Main Ideas

Check (✔) the two main ideas of the reading.

_____ 1. People all over the world have made beautiful and useful pottery for thousands of years.

_____ 2. The Egyptians were the first to decorate their pottery.

_____ 3. Pottery is made by shaping, glazing, and firing clay.

_____ 4. Some pottery is very fragile and expensive and can be seen in museums.

WRITING

Look around your home and school. What kinds of pottery and ceramics do you see? Make lists of the things that you notice. Compare your lists with other students.

Examples of pottery	Examples of other ceramics

WORD STUDY

A. Irregular Verbs

Study the irregular verbs in this list. Then choose the correct verb form to complete each sentence. Use a verb from line 1 in sentence 1, and so on.

Present	Past	Past Participle
1. shoot	shot	shot
2. eat	ate	eaten
3. freeze	froze	frozen
4. hide	hid	hidden
5. hold	held	held
6. steal	stole	stolen

1. The comet _____*shot*_____ through the dark night sky like a rocket.

2. Are you hungry? Have you _____ anything yet today?

3. Be careful outside today. Last night was very cold, and now all the water from yesterday's rain has _____. Ice is everywhere.

4. The entrances to many caves are _____ underground or underwater. They are very hard to find.

5. Could you _____ my books for me for a minute? I have to make a quick phone call.

6. While I was looking the other way, a squirrel ran up and _____ half of my sandwich at the picnic Saturday. Everyone thought it was really funny.

B. Prepositions

Complete the paragraphs with the correct prepositions.

A variety (1) __*of*__ useful and artistic objects made (2) _____ clay can be called pottery. Pottery is part (3) _____ the larger family (4) _____ ceramics. Ceramics are materials other than metals or plastics that are made (5) _____ people. Bricks and tiles are two examples (6) _____ ceramics.

Pottery developed (7) _____ many places around the world (8) _____ many different times (9) _____ history. Styles (10) _____ one region often influenced another. Pottery making began around 7,000 years ago (11) _____ Egypt and the Middle East. The earliest forms (12) _____ pottery were objects (13) _____ use (14) _____ the house, such as large vases (15) _____ holding water.

BUILDING VOCABULARY SKILLS

A. Vocabulary Review

Match the words in column A with their meanings in column B.

A	B
_____ 1. coastal	a. area
_____ 2. entrance	b. very real, lifelike
_____ 3. prehistoric	c. gets out of
_____ 4. realistic	d. think about
_____ 5. border	e. before history
_____ 6. ancient	f. a way to go in
_____ 7. region	g. near the sea
_____ 8. escapes	h. go in the opposite direction
_____ 9. reverse	i. a line that divides two countries
_____ 10. consider	j. very, very old

B. Context Clues

Tell the meaning of each word in bold print. Use context clues.

1. Some trees are white when you look at them. They have white **bark** outside. American Indians used this white **bark** to make canoes, or small boats, to use on rivers and lakes. They also used it for paintings and writing.

2. I didn't **realize** that today was Saturday until I looked at the calendar this morning. I was glad!

3. Most houses in the United States and Canada have **screens** on the doors and windows. **Screens** help keep bugs outside, but they let fresh air into the house.

4. Mark wants to go to the football game **whether** it's raining or not. I would rather stay home if it rains. Mark doesn't care at all about the weather. He'll go no matter what.

Paper

Pre-reading

1. How is paper made?
2. When did people first begin to use paper?
3. What things do people use every day that are made of paper?

Paper is everywhere. We use it for homework, money, checks, books, letters, wallpaper, and greeting cards. We have paper towels, napkins, plates, cups, and tissues. We print the news every day on newspaper. Our history and knowledge is written on paper. Without paper, our lives would be completely
5 different.

From the very beginning of time, people have tried to record their thoughts and lives. The earliest humans drew pictures on cave walls. Later, people used large pieces of clay to write on. Almost 5,000 years ago, the Egyptians wrote on pieces of plants called *papyrus.* Papyrus was used throughout the

10 ancient world of the Mediterranean for thousands of years. Eventually it was
replaced by parchment. Parchment was made from animal skins. It was
stronger and lasted longer than any other material.

The Chinese made the first real paper in the year A.D. 105. They mixed tree
bark and small pieces of old cloth with water. They used a screen to remove
15 the thin, wet piece of paper. Then they let the paper dry in the Sun. The
Chinese kept papermaking a secret until after 751. In that year there was a war
between the Chinese and the Muslims. Many Chinese papermakers were
taken away from China to live in Muslim countries. The art of papermaking
soon spread throughout the Muslim world. Finally, by the end of the twelfth
20 century, papermaking reached Europe. The first paper made in Europe was in
Spain in 1151.

The first important improvement on the Chinese method of papermaking
was in France in 1798. A man named Nicholas Louis Robert invented a
machine for making paper. His machine could make paper much faster than
25 one person could by hand. However, his machine was not very successful.
About ten years later an Englishman improved on Robert's machine and began
producing paper.

The most important improvement in papermaking also happened in France.
A scientist observed a wasp making its nest. The wasp chewed up pieces of
30 wood, mixed it with the chemicals in its mouth, and made a paper nest. The
scientist realized that people could make paper from wood, too. Finally, a
machine was invented for grinding wood into pulp to use for making paper.

Today, the principal ingredient in paper is wood pulp. It is made by
machine. There are also other kinds of paper made from rice, wheat, cotton,
35 corn, and other plants. Paper from wood pulp is the most common. Canada
and the United States are the world leaders in paper production, due in part
to the quantity of wood that is available in the forests of these two countries.

Because paper is made of wood, many people are becoming concerned that
too many trees are being chopped down every year in order to produce paper.
40 Trees are an important part of the environment. As a result, many companies
that produce paper are using old paper instead of new wood pulp to make
paper. This method of using old products again instead of simply throwing
them away is called *recycling*. Recycling paper helps reduce the number of
trees that are used every year. Many people also try to use less paper in their
45 daily lives. They use both sides of a sheet of paper instead of just one. They

use cloth handkerchiefs instead of paper tissues. There are also special containers in many schools and public places where people can put used paper instead of throwing it into the garbage can. Then this paper is collected to be recycled.

50   Whether we use a little or a lot, paper has an important place in our lives. The books we read and write are made of paper. Our history and scientific inventions have all been recorded on paper. This, however, is changing. Other methods of storing information are becoming common. Computers can store an enormous amount of information in a much smaller space. Computer faxes,

55 electronic mail, and the Internet are only three examples of technology that have replaced paper. Who knows, perhaps one day people will not use paper to write at all!

WORKING WITH VOCABULARY

A. Focus on the Reading

Choose the best word or phrase for each sentence.

available	enormous	principal	recycling
bark	improvement	pulp	screen
chopped down	method	realized	whether

1. The Chinese made the first real paper in the year A.D. 105. They mixed tree _____ and small pieces of old cloth with water.

2. They used a _____ to remove the thin, wet piece of paper.

3. A scientist observed a wasp making its nest. The wasp chewed up pieces of wood, mixed it with chemicals in its mouth, and made a paper nest. The scientist _____ that people could make paper from wood, too.

4. Today, the principal ingredient in paper is wood _____.

5. Canada and the United States are the world leaders in paper production, due in part to the quantity of wood that is _____ in the forests of these two countries.

6. Because paper is made of wood, many people are becoming concerned that too many trees are being ———————————— every year in order to produce paper.

7. As a result, many companies that produce paper are using old paper instead of new wood pulp to make paper. This ———————————— of using old products again instead of simply throwing them away is called recycling.

8. ———————————— paper helps reduce the number of trees that are used every year.

9. ———————————— we use a little or a lot, paper has an important place in our lives.

10. This, however, is changing. Other methods of storing information are becoming common. Computers can store an ———————————— amount of information in a much smaller space.

B. Focus on the Reading

Choose the best word or phrase for each sentence.

available	enormous	principal	recycling
bark	improvement	pulp	screen
chopped down	method	realized	whether

1. A bee flew into the kitchen through a hole in the ———————————— on the window.

2. Dinosaurs were ———————————— animals. They weighed thousands of kilograms.

3. Reading is just one ———————————— of relaxing. Some people prefer to watch TV, take a walk, or just take a nap. Exercising is also a good way to relax.

4. _____ is becoming more common all over the world. Most big cities ask people to separate their garbage into metal, plastic, glass, and paper. This really helps the environment.

5. I wanted to have my hair cut on Tuesday, but my hairdresser was not _____. She always takes the day off on Tuesday, so I made the appointment for Wednesday.

6. Cacao is the _____ ingredient in milk chocolate. The other ingredients are milk, sugar, and vanilla.

7. After the taxi had driven out of sight, Patty _____ that she left her suitcase in the trunk! She called the taxi company when she got home, and they returned it to her.

UNDERSTANDING THE READING

A. Comprehension Questions

Answer the questions about the reading.

1. Name five things that are made from paper.
2. What is paper made from?
3. Who invented paper?
4. What did people write on before paper? Name three things.
5. What was the first important improvement on the Chinese method of papermaking?
6. How did a wasp help a French scientist learn about making paper?
*7. Why are people worried about making a lot of paper?
8. What is recycling?
*9. What else do people recycle?
*10. How might paper disappear in the future?

B. Details

Write **T** if the sentence is true and **F** if it is false.

_____ 1. Papyrus is a plant that ancient Egyptians wrote on.

_____ 2. Before papyrus, people used large pieces of clay to write on.

_____ 3. Parchment is not as strong as papyrus.

_____ 4. There was a war between the Chinese and the Muslims in A.D. 105.

_____ 5. Paper was made in Europe for the first time in 1151 in Spain.

_____ 6. Paper can also be made from rice, wheat, cotton, corn, and other plants.

_____ 7. Electronic mail is one example of how technology has replaced paper.

C. Main Ideas

Check (✔) the two main ideas of the reading.

_____ 1. Throughout history, people have always found new materials to write on.

_____ 2. The Chinese kept papermaking a secret until A.D. 751.

_____ 3. Paper is an important part of our life, but technology is changing this fast.

_____ 4. Many people recycle paper in order to save trees.

WRITING

Do people recycle paper and other materials in your country? Write a few sentences to explain how you recycle these things. Then compare your information with other students.

Paper   Glass
Metal   Plastic

WORD STUDY

A. Suffixes

In English, you can often change an adjective to a noun by adding **-y, -ty,** or **-ity.**

Look at the adjectives in the chart. Add the correct suffix to each one and make a noun.

Spelling note: If a word ends in e, drop the e before adding -ity.

-Y			-ITY	
Adjective	**Noun**		**Adjective**	**Noun**
difficult	_____		similar	_____
			equal	_____
-TY			popular	_____
Adjective	**Noun**		human	_____
special	_____		electric	_____
certain	_____		able	_____
safe	_____			

Choose the best noun from the chart for each sentence.

1. Marie is a chef. She went to cooking school. Her _____*specialty*_____ is desserts. They are so delicious! You should go to her restaurant and try some of them.

2. The _____ of chocolate spread all over Europe. People loved it!

3. I am having _____ with my English homework. Could you help me?

4. There are many _____ between the coffee plant and the cacao plant. For example, both grow in hot climates and produce pretty flowers and beans.

5. It is a law in the United States for people to wear seat belts in cars. The law was written for everyone's _____. It saves lives.

6. Olympic athletes have great athletic _____. They train very hard for many years before they go to the Olympic Games.

7. UNICEF works with governments to develop programs that will improve the lives of all _____, especially children.

B. Suffixes

In English, we can add **-y** to some nouns to make adjectives.

Look at the example:

Noun + **-y** = adjective

rain + **-y** = rainy

Yesterday was a **rainy** day.

Spelling Notes:

1. *If a noun ends in silent **e**, drop the **e** before adding **-y**.*
2. *If a noun ends in consonant-vowel-consonant and is a one-syllable word, double the final consonant before adding **-y**.*

Here are two examples:

ice (drop the **e**) → **icy**

sun (double the **n**) → **sunny**

Add **-y** to each noun to make an adjective. Remember to follow the spelling rules. Then choose the best adjective for each sentence.

fun _____*funny*_____   juice _____

dirt _____   wind _____

cloud _____

1. The temperature was below freezing last night, and today the streets are _____*icy*_____.

2. The weather today is also bad. It's very _____ and the sky is _____.

3. Fresh fruit is so delicious! I especially like oranges. They are so

   _____.

4. Yesterday our teacher told us a story. It was very _____,
   and we laughed together for a long time.

BUILDING VOCABULARY SKILLS

A. Vocabulary Review

Match the words in column A with their meanings in column B.

A	B
____ 1. delicious	a. directions for cooking
____ 2. originally	b. quantity
____ 3. melt	c. in the beginning
____ 4. gather	d. change to a liquid
____ 5. amount	e. change to ice
____ 6. illness	f. tastes very good
____ 7. freeze	g. bad health
____ 8. recipe	h. collect

B. Context Clues

Tell the meaning of each word in bold print. Use context clues.

1. My mother has a beautiful **jewelry** box on her dresser. She keeps her rings, necklaces, and earrings inside of it.

2. The ancient Chinese **advanced** pottery making to a beautiful art. People before them had simply made useful objects, like pots and bowls. The Chinese made the best pottery in history.

3. If you leave your bicycle out in the rain, it might **rust. Rust** will turn your bike orange and make holes in it. You should try to keep it out of the rain.

4. Do you have any **coins?** I need to make a phone call, and I only have a dollar bill.

5. The workmen next door **hammered** on the roof of the new building all day yesterday. The noise of the **hammering** gave me a terrible headache.

Pre-reading

1. What is silver?
2. What do people make from silver?
3. Why do people like silver?

People have always loved silver jewelry, containers, and other objects. Museums have large collections of ancient silver pieces. Some of them are from Egypt and are almost six thousand years old. Persia and other Asian countries have also made beautiful silver objects for centuries. The Romans
5   learned from them and then greatly advanced the art and science of working with silver. Spanish explorers found that the native Indians of Central and South America also had a beautiful tradition of making silver jewelry.

    Silver (Ag) is one of the most valuable metals in the world. It is valuable for four principal reasons. First, silver is a rare metal, which means that there

10   isn't very much of it in the world compared to most other metals. Second, it is a beautiful white, shiny color. Because of its appearance, people use silver to make jewelry and other beautiful objects. Third, silver is easy to work with, so people can make many things from it without a lot of difficulty. It can be easily melted, bent, or shaped in other ways. Fourth, silver does not rust, or
15   oxidize, when it is left in the air and rain. Some metals, such as copper (Cu), will turn blue when the oxygen of the air touches them for a long time. This does not happen with silver.

The most important use of silver is for making money. Governments have used silver to make coins for centuries. Jewelry, dishes, and other containers
20   have also been important uses of silver. Silver is used to make mirrors. If it is applied to the back of a sheet of glass, the glass becomes a mirror. Today silver is also used in chemical and electrical engineering because electricity can travel easily through silver, and it does not rust. This makes it a very good material for wires and important parts of airplane and train engines. Another
25   important use of silver is in medicine; dentists, for example, use silver to fill teeth that have holes in them. Silver is also very important in photography. It is used in many kinds of film and material for developing film.

Silver is very popular because it is so easy to work with. It can be hammered into a very thin sheet, less than 0.00025 millimeters! Only gold is
30   easier to work with than silver. Silver is also a soft metal, usually too soft by itself to be used for coins. Most often, it is mixed with copper. A small quantity of copper strengthens silver, but does not change the color.

Silver is widely distributed throughout the world, but in small amounts. It is usually found mixed with other metals in the stone of mountains,
35   underground, and sometimes in the soil underwater. In order to remove silver in the past, people had to work very hard. Technology has made silver mining easier. There are now chemical processes and other complicated processes that will separate silver from other metals. The United States, Mexico, Canada, Peru, and Australia are the leading silver-producing countries in the
40   world. About half of all the world's silver is produced by North and South America together.

Metals are very important to a society. Each time people discovered a new metal or invented new ways to use metals they already had, their society advanced. Modern society could not exist without metals. We need them to
45   make our lives work.

Silver is a very special metal. It has many uses for people in the simplest and the most complex societies. It is also very beautiful and has enabled people to make objects that have lasted for thousands of years.

WORKING WITH VOCABULARY

A. Focus on the Reading

Choose the best word for each sentence.

advanced	coins	distributed	jewelry
appearance	compared	exist	rare
bent	complex	hammered	rust

1. People have always loved silver _____, containers, and other objects.

2. Persia and other Asian countries have also made beautiful silver objects for centuries. The Romans learned from them and then greatly _____ the art and science of working with silver.

3. Silver is valuable for four principal reasons. First, silver is a _____ metal, which means there isn't very much of it in the world _____ to most other metals.

4. Second, it is a beautiful white, shiny color. Because of its _____, people use silver to make jewelry and other beautiful objects.

5. Third, silver is easy to work with, so people can make many things from it without a lot of difficulty. It can be easily melted, _____, or shaped in other ways.

6. Fourth, silver does not _____, or oxidize, when it is left in the air and rain.

7. Silver is very popular because it is very easy to work with. It can be _____ into a very thin sheet, less than 0.00025 millimeters.

8. Silver is widely _____ throughout the world, but in small amounts. It is usually found mixed with other metals in the stone of mountains, underground, and sometimes in the soil underwater.

9. Modern society could not _____ without metals. We need them to make our lives work.

10. Silver is a very special metal. It has many uses for people in the simplest and the most _____ societies.

B. Focus on New Contexts

Choose the best word for each sentence.

advanced	coins	distributes	jewelry
appearance	compared	exist	rare
bent	complex	hammered	rust

1. Diamonds and rubies are two very beautiful stones. Both of them are very _____ —they are not easy to find in the world. Because of this, they are very expensive.

2. The weather in Miami is very warm, especially _____ to Chicago, where it's usually cold.

3. When people began to use wood pulp for making paper, the process _____ greatly.

4. Do squirrels _____ in your native country? They live throughout North America.

5. Hangers are made from wire that is _____ into a special shape for hanging clothes.

6. Look at that car. It's all orange and covered with _____. It must be very old.

7. During times of emergency, UNICEF _____ food and water to victims.

8. People make necklaces, rings, and other _____ from silver and gold because of their beautiful _____.

UNDERSTANDING THE READING

A. Comprehension Questions

Answer the questions about the reading.

1. How long have people used silver?

2. Why is silver so valuable? Give four reasons.

3. What is the most important use of silver?

4. How is silver made stronger?

5. What are some other uses of silver?

6. What is rust, or oxidation?

7. Where is silver found in the world?

8. Why is silver rare?

*9. Is clay rare? Why or why not?

*10. How is silver used differently in simple and complex societies?

B. Details

Circle the letter of the best answer.

1. Persia and other Asian countries

   a. are leading producers of silver.

   b. took silver from Egypt.

   c. don't have silver coins.

   d. made beautiful silver objects for centuries.

2. The ancient Romans

   a. preferred to use gold.

   b. didn't use silver.

   c. explored Central and South America.

   d. greatly advanced the art and science of silver making.

3. Silver is valuable because
   a. it is easy to find.
   b. there isn't very much of it.
   c. it comes from many parts of the world.
   d. it is mixed with copper sometimes.

4. The oxygen in the air does not cause silver to
   a. bend.   c. freeze.
   b. shine.   d. rust.

5. Silver is a very good material for wires because
   a. it can easily be melted.
   b. of its shiny appearance.
   c. it can be hammered into a thin sheet.
   d. electricity can travel easily through it.

6. Silver
   a. can only last 500 years.
   b. oxidizes from the air.
   c. is not used in simple societies.
   d. is beautiful and useful.

C. Main Ideas

Check (✔) the two main ideas of the reading.

_____ 1. Silver is used in medicine, engineering, and photography.

_____ 2. Modern society could not exist without metals.

_____ 3. Silver is a beautiful metal with many important uses in society.

_____ 4. Technology has made silver mining easier.

_____ 5. There is not a lot of silver in the world, so it is rare and valuable.

WRITING

Two other very rare and valuable metals are gold and platinum. Look in an encyclopedia to find some information about one of these two metals. Then write a short paragraph about some of the uses of this metal, where it is found, or its history in society. Be sure to use your own words. Do not copy sentences from the encyclopedia. When you finish, compare your information in class.

WORD STUDY

A. Suffixes

Several words in English end in the suffix **-ever.** Look at these words and their meanings. Then choose the best word for each sentence.

whatever = "anything"   **whenever** = "any time"

whoever = "anyone"   **wherever** = "any place"

1. Please come and visit me _____*whenever*_____ you like. You can come at any time.

2. We can go _____ you'd like tonight. We could go to the movies, to a party, or to a restaurant for dinner. It's your choice.

3. Shopping malls in North America are enormous. There are so many stores in one place that you can buy _____ you'd like all at the same time. It's very convenient for shoppers.

4. _____ would like to go on the trip to the museum next week should give his or her name to the teacher today so she can make arrangements. I'm going for sure. Are you?

B. Irregular Verbs

Study the irregular verbs in this list. Then choose the correct verb form to complete each sentence. Use a verb from line 1 in sentence 1, and so on. Remember to make each verb agree with its subject.

Present	Past	Past Participle
1. bend	bent	bent
2. hurt	hurt	hurt
3. lend	lent	lent
4. break	broke	broken
5. wake	woke	woken
6. ride	rode	ridden

1. Silver is a very useful metal. It can easily be _____*bent*_____, and it never rusts.

2. Silver mines can be very dangerous. People must take care not to get _____ when they are in them.

3. I _____ my favorite pen to someone in the class yesterday, and today she forgot to give it back. I'll have to ask her about it tomorrow.

4. Porcelain is very fragile. It _____ easily. People must handle it carefully.

5. Anna usually _____ up early in the morning, around 6:45.

6. Have you ever _____ on an elephant or a camel? It looks very difficult, but also fun!

BUILDING VOCABULARY SKILLS

A. Vocabulary Review

Match the words in column A with their opposites in column B.

A   B

_____ 1. principal   a. sweet

_____ 2. fragile   b. ugly

_____ 3. humid   c. permanent

_____ 4. delicious   d. not important

_____ 5. attractive   e. terrible

_____ 6. complex   f. strong

_____ 7. bitter   g. dry

_____ 8. temporary   h. simple

B. Context Clues

Choose the answer that is closest in meaning to each word in bold print. Use context clues.

1. Mary's family has been in Canada for centuries. Her **ancestors** first arrived in Canada in the 1500s from Europe.

    a. grandparents   c. relatives from long ago

    b. parents   d. friends and neighbors

2. My parents think about life differently than I do. They are very traditional, but I am more modern. We are different because we were born in two different **generations**. In fact, my grandparents' **generation** was probably very strange to my parents when they were young.

    a. brothers and sisters   c. traditions

    b. one lifetime   d. places

3. Some people think the Maya and Aztec Indians of Central America were **primitive** people. The truth is that their societies were very complex and advanced.

   a. advanced
   b. private
   c. simple
   d. difficult

4. There were many Indian **tribes** in the United States and Canada many years ago. The Cherokee, Sioux, Apache, and Cree are four examples. These Indian **tribes** lived in different regions across North America.

   a. names of people
   b. groups of people
   c. American cities
   d. places where Indians lived

5. Some men like to wear **beards** and mustaches on their faces. Other men shave every day because they don't want to have hair on their faces.

   a. hair above the top lip
   b. hair on the chin and cheeks
   c. long hair on the head
   d. hair above the eyes

Unit 24

Australian Aborigines

Northern Territory
Queensland
South Pacific Ocean
Western Australia
South Australia
New South Wales
Victoria
Indian Ocean
Tasmania

Pre-reading

1. Who are the native people of Australia?
2. What do they look like?
3. What do you know about their life and culture?

The Australian Aborigines are the native people of Australia. They have dark wavy hair, brown eyes, and dark brown skin. Many of the men wear beards. Aborigines are tall and slender people. In 1788, when the Europeans first went to Australia to live, there were about 750,000 Aborigines there. They
5   were divided into 500 tribes, each with its own language. Each tribe was a related family group and lived in its own area of the country.

Some scientists believe that the ancestors of the Aborigines arrived in Australia almost 50,000 years ago. No one knows for sure, but they probably came from the mountains of Southeast Asia. Many people think that Australia

10   was once connected to Asia by a land bridge. The Aborigines traveled south
by land. Later, there were changes in the Earth and the land between Australia
and Asia became islands surrounded by water. The Aborigines were cut off
from the rest of the world for thousands of years.

Life was very difficult in Australia. The climate is very hot and dry, and
15   much of the land is desert. However, the Aborigines learned to live there.
They hunted animals and caught fish from the ocean. They gathered wild
fruits and vegetables, birds' eggs, and shellfish. They made tools out of wood
and stone to help them hunt, cook, and grow plants. One of these tools is
called a *boomerang.* It is a piece of curved wood used for hunting and
20   fighting. When someone throws a boomerang, it flies for a distance, then turns
and comes back to the person who threw it.

The Aborigines did not have permanent villages. They moved from place to
place looking for new supplies of food. They made huts out of tree branches
and grass, or found shelter under very large rocks. The Aborigines always
25   stayed together as family groups. They thought that family relationships were
very important. Both men and women had important roles in their societies.

The Aborigines have always had a rich tradition of art. Thousands of years
ago they began painting pictures on cave walls. They painted on tree bark.
They carved figures from wood and stone and painted them. These traditions
30   continue today. The art of the Aborigines is imaginative and religious. The
Aborigines believe that their ancestors, thousands and thousands of years ago,
created the world. They believe that these beings never died—they became
part of nature and will live forever. In this way, all of nature is special to the
Aborigines because they see their own histories in the life all around them.
35   The Aborigines call this story of creation the "Dreaming." Each family has a
story of its own beginning. It explains who the family is and what part of the
land they came from. Aborigines tell this story from generation to generation.
The Dreaming is very important to them, and helps them see who they are
and where they came from. They also explain their stories in their painting.
40   Aborigines make beautiful and brightly colored paintings. Each one tells the
Dreaming of a family.

Today Aborigines are Australian citizens. There are about 206,000
Aborigines in Australia, which is about one percent of the population. Some
of them work and live in Australia's big cities. Others remain with their tribes
45   in desert and coastal communities. Some people think that Aborigines are

very primitive people who don't like modern society. These people are wrong. Aborigines have an old and unique culture that they want to preserve. Many still dress in traditional style with beautiful decorations. Many Aboriginal artists continue the tradition of Aboriginal painting and telling the Dreaming.

WORKING WITH VOCABULARY

A. Focus on the Reading

Choose the best word for each sentence.

ancestors	generation	relationships	slender
beards	huts	shellfish	tribes
Dreaming	primitive	shelter	wavy

1. The Australian Aborigines are the native people of Australia. They have dark _____ hair, brown eyes, and dark brown skin.

2. Aborigines are tall and _____ people.

3. In 1788, when the Europeans first went to Australia to live, there were about 750,000 Aborigines there. They were divided into 500 _____ , each with its own language.

4. Some scientists believe that the _____ of the Aborigines arrived in Australia almost 50,000 years ago.

5. The Aborigines did not have permanent villages. They moved from place to place looking for new supplies of food. They made _____ out of tree branches and grass, or found _____ under very large rocks.

6. The Aborigines always stayed together as family groups. They thought that family _____ were very important.

7. Each family has a story of its own beginning. It explains who the family is and what part of the land they came from. Aborigines tell this story from _____ to _____ .

8. Some people think that Aborigines are very _____ people who don't like modern society. These people are wrong.

B. Focus on New Contexts

Choose the best word for each sentence.

ancestors	generation	relationships	slender
beards	huts	shellfish	tribes
Dreaming	primitive	shelter	wavy

1. Many restaurants along the coast specialize in seafood. They serve fresh fish and _____ such as oysters and clams.

2. Archaeologists believe that the _____ drawings found in caves in France are tens of thousands of years old.

3. When the sea becomes very rough with high waves, most smaller boats find _____ in the harbors. The waves are smaller there, and the wind is not as strong.

4. One of my brothers has straight black hair, and the other has _____ blond hair. They are exact opposites of each other!

5. Many beautiful Aboriginal paintings explain the _____. This is what the Aborigines call the creation of their world and their own spiritual history.

6. Richard is very tall and _____. He looks like a professional basketball player.

7. Many customs change from one _____ to another. Parents and their children often don't live the same kind of life because of the difference in their ages.

8. Anne is American, but her _____ are from Germany and Ireland. They moved to the United States two generations ago.

UNDERSTANDING THE READING

A. Comprehension Questions

Answer the questions about the reading.

1. Who are the native people of Australia? Describe them.

2. How many Aborigines were there in Australia originally?

3. Where did they come from?

4. How did they arrive in Australia?

5. What was life like in Australia for the Aborigines?

6. What is a boomerang?

7. What kind of art do the Aborigines have?

8. What is the Dreaming?

B. Details

Write **T** if the sentence is true and **F** if it is false.

_____ 1. Most Aborigines have straight dark hair.

_____ 2. The Europeans first went to Australia to live in 1788.

_____ 3. The Aborigines had one language and 500 tribes.

_____ 4. The Aborigines probably went to Australia from Asia by boat.

_____ 5. Aborigines did not have permanent villages. They often moved in search of food.

_____ 6. Families are very important in the Aborigine culture.

_____ 7. The Aborigines do not have a very strong tradition of art.

_____ 8. The Aborigines are very primitive people who don't like modern society.

C. Main Ideas

Check (✔) the two main ideas of the reading.

_____ 1. Aborigines are the original people of Australia and have lived there for thousands of years.

_____ 2. Aborigines lived in the desert and hunted animals.

_____ 3. Aborigines lived in tribes of related family groups.

_____ 4. Aborigines have a long tradition of art that mixes religion and history together.

WRITING

The Aborigines make paintings that explain the history of their ancestors. These pictures tell a story. Try to make a picture that explains your own history. It can be funny or serious. Be prepared to tell the story that your picture is about!

WORD STUDY

A. Noun Substitutes

Read these groups of sentences and study the pronouns in bold print. Circle the noun or noun phrase that each pronoun replaces.

1. Some scientists believe that the (ancestors of the Aborigines) arrived in Australia almost 50,000 years ago. No one knows for sure, but **they** probably came from the mountains of Southeast Asia.

2. Aborigines made tools out of wood and stone to help them hunt, cook, and grow plants. One of these tools is called a *boomerang*. **It** is a piece of curved wood used for hunting and fighting. When someone throws a boomerang, **it** flies for a distance, then turns and comes back to the person who threw **it.**

3. The Aborigines believe that their ancestors, thousands and thousands of years ago, created the world. They believe that these beings never died— **they** became part of nature and will live forever.

4. Each family has a story of its own beginning. **It** explains who the family is and what part of the land they came from.

B. Suffixes

In English, we can add the suffixes **-ous** and **-like** to some nouns to make adjectives. Words that end in **-ous** mean "full of something."
Here is an example:

Silver mines can be very **dangerous** places to work. (full of danger)
Words that end in **-like** mean "similar to," or "like."
Here is an example:

Sometimes adults behave in very **childlike** ways. (like a child)
Spelling Notes:

1. *If a noun ends in silent e, drop the e before adding the suffix **-ous**. There are no spelling changes when you add the suffix **-like**.*

2. *If a noun ends in **y**, change the **y** to **i** before adding **-ous**.*

Add the corrrect suffix to each noun in the chart.

-OUS		-LIKE	
Nouns	**Adjectives**	**Nouns**	**Adjectives**
joy	*joyous*	life	
fame		child	
danger		war	
mystery			

Now choose the best adjective to complete each sentence.

1. Some cave paintings of animals are very _____*lifelike*_____. The animals look real.

2. Christopher Colombus was a _____ explorer. Most people around the world know who he was and what areas he explored.

3. Have you ever heard of the Devil's Triangle? It's a very _____ place in the Atlantic and Caribbean Oceans where ships and planes disappear, and no one knows why.

4. Birthdays and weddings are _____ days. People sing and dance and really enjoy themselves.

5. Only some of the North American Indian tribes were _____.

BUILDING VOCABULARY SKILLS

A. Vocabulary Review

Circle the word that does not belong with the other words. Tell why the other three words go together.

1. object, thing, coin, item
2. copper, gold, silver, paper
3. divide, connect, join, attach
4. cotton, tree, rice, beans
5. damage, destroy, harm, create
6. bark, branch, wasp, leaf
7. major, simple, principal, important

B. Context Clues

Tell the meaning of each word in bold print. Use context clues.

1. John is really **fascinated** by computers. He works with them and reads about them all the time.
2. One of the **advantages** of living in a big city is that there are so many interesting things to do night and day. Small cities don't have that advantage.
3. Satellites are **controlled** from a control station back on Earth. The people in the station use computers to **control** the movement of the satellite and the information it sends and receives.
4. Most supermarkets in the United States have **automatic** doors at the entrance. The doors open **automatically** when someone is near the door. This makes it easier for shoppers to go in and out with their carts.
5. Some animals can be trained to **perform** many different actions. For example, dogs can learn to do things such as sit, lie down, and shake people's hands.

Unit 25

Robots

Pre-reading

1. What are robots?
2. Where and how are robots used?
3. What place do you think robots will have in the future?

People are fascinated by robots. Science fiction books and movies feed people's imaginations, making them wonder about the possibilities of robots living and working with them. Is it possible for robots to look like people, work like people, and think like people? In the future, anything is possible.
5   Already today there are tens of thousands of robots doing work all over the world.

   Robot is the name given to any machine that can do a certain job automatically. These machines come in many shapes and sizes. It is possible to build a robot in the shape of a person, but most look like machines built for

10   specific purposes. They are controlled or operated by computers. The computers tell the robot what to do and how to do it. People write the programs for the computers that control the robots. There are several important differences between robots and regular machines run by computers. Robots can function by themselves, without people. Robots can sense the
15   environment around them and respond to it. They can adapt, or change, while they are working. Robots can also complete several steps in a process and can try other methods if one does not work. Ordinary machines cannot do these things.

Serious research began on robots in the 1950s and 1960s in several
20   countries. The first real robot was put to work in 1961 in a General Motors car factory in the United States. This robot performed a job that was too dangerous for people. At the same time in Japan, a robot was used to put together watches in a watch factory. These robots did not look like mechanical people. They looked like complex machines made of metal and computers.
25   Later, robots became more complex and could be made to do more difficult work.

One of the greatest advantages of robots is that they can work in situations that are dangerous or harmful for human workers. For example, the continuous smell of paint has a harmful effect on painters, but it doesn't
30   bother a robot. Robots can work in nuclear power plants and in undersea research stations that might be dangerous for humans. Already, robots are working in the plastics industry and in chemical and industrial equipment industries. One of the most common uses of robots is still in automobile factories. They can do the heavy, unpleasant, or dangerous work. For
35   example, a computer programmer writes a program for a robot that tells how much paint to use, how thick is must be, and the size of the car body. The robot does not waste any time or movements. It never becomes bored. It never wants to take a break for lunch. It can last 20 to 25 years. These kinds of industrial robots are not usually mobile. The work they need to do is brought
40   to them, like cars on an assembly line, for example.

The robot industry is a big business. By the middle of the 1990s, Japan led the world in robot production with more than 71,000 industrial robots at work. Both the United States and Japan, as well as other countries, continue to develop more advanced robots. Robots can now be made to perform more
45   complex jobs. Robots can make decisions while they are working and learn

from their mistakes. Robots can now see with TV camera "eyes." They can easily hear and can even speak using a voice made by a computer. But it is difficult to make a robot "understand." Thinking and understanding are very
50 human qualities. The robots of the future will probably be very complex. They will be able to perform many humanlike tasks. Robots and other technology will make the future a very interesting place!

WORKING WITH VOCABULARY

A. Focus on the Reading

Choose the best word for each sentence.

adapt	controlled	mobile	qualities
advantages	fascinated	performed	specific
automatically	function	programs	tasks

1. People are _____ by robots. Science fiction books and movies feed people's imagination, making them wonder about the possibilities of robots living and working with them.

2. *Robot* is the name given to any machine that can do a certain job _____.

3. These machines come in many shapes and sizes. It is possible to build a robot in the shape of a person, but most look like machines built for a _____ purpose.

4. They are _____ or operated by computers. The computers tell the robot what to do and how to do it.

5. People write the _____ for the computers that control the robots.

6. There are several important differences between robots and regular machines run by computers. Robots can _____ by themselves, without people.

7. Robots can sense the environment around them and respond to it. They
   can _____, or change, while they are working.

8. The first real robot was put to work in 1961 in a General Motors car
   factory in the United States. This robot _____ a job that
   was too dangerous for people.

9. It is difficult to make a robot "understand." Thinking and understanding
   are very human _____.

10. The robots of the future will probably be very complex. They will be able
    to perform many humanlike _____. Robots and
    technology will make the future a very interesting place!

B. Focus on New Contexts

Choose the best word for each sentence.

adapt	control	mobile	qualities
advantages	fascinated	perform	specific
automatically	function	program	tasks

1. Many people believe that honesty and sincerity are two of the most
   important human _____. What do you think?

2. There are many _____ to going to a foreign country to
   study. First, you will learn to speak the language. Second, you can make
   many interesting friends from all over the world.

3. Sometimes it is hard to _____ to a new environment. You
   must learn to change your lifestyle and sometimes your way of thinking if
   you want to feel comfortable.

4. People from my grandmother's generation don't really understand how
   robots and computers _____. Our new technology is a
   mystery to them.

5. Martha can ————————————— her computer to pay her bills, send
   mail, and receive faxes.

6. One day, robots may be able to perform household —————————————,
   such as doing the laundry, cleaning the house, and cooking meals. That
   would be great!

7. Susan is ————————————— by Hollywood. She always goes to the
   movies, collects pictures of famous movie stars, and wants to become an
   actress some day.

UNDERSTANDING THE READING

A. Comprehension Questions

Answer the questions about the reading.

1. What is a robot?

2. How are robots controlled?

3. What are the differences between robots and regular machines?

4. When did the first robot go to work?

5. What was its job?

6. What do robots look like?

7. What is one of the greatest advantages of using robots for work?

8. What is one of the most common places for a robot to work?

9. How many robots did Japan have in the middle of the 1990s?

*10. What will the robots of the future be able to do?

B. Details

Write **T** if the sentence is true and **F** if it is false.

_____ 1. Robots are machines that can work automatically.

_____ 2. Robots can be built to look something like people.

_____ 3. Most robots look like complex machines with computers.

_____ 4. Robots cannot adapt, or change, while they are working.

_____ 5. The first robot went to work in Japan in the 1950s.

_____ 6. Industrial robots are usually mobile.

_____ 7. Robots can see, hear, and speak.

_____ *8. Robots can also understand.

C. Main Ideas

Check (✔) the two main ideas of the reading.

_____ 1. Science fiction books and movies feed people's imagination about robots.

_____ 2. Robots are complex, computerized machines that work automatically.

_____ 3. Robots usually don't look like mechanical people.

_____ 4. Robots are very useful because they can do dangerous work that humans can't do.

_____ 5. The robots of the future will be even more advanced.

WRITING

Have you ever wished you had a robot to do something for you? Imagine that you could have a robot designed just for you. What would you want the robot to do? Write a description of your robot. Explain what tasks it will perform. Draw a picture of it if you like! When you finish, tell your classmates about your robot.

WORD STUDY

A. Word Forms

Study the list of verbs, nouns, and adjectives. Notice how they are related to each other. Then choose the correct word for each sentence. Use a word from line 1 in sentence 1, and so on. Make the nouns plural if necessary.

VERB	NOUN	ADJECTIVE
1. describe	description	descriptive
2. separate	separation	separate
3. educate	education	(un)educated
4. accept	acceptance	(un)acceptable
5. realize	realization	—
6. advance	advancement	advanced
7. value	value	valuable
8. exist	existence	—
9. fascinate	fascination	fascinating
10. replace	replacement	—

1. Paul gave the police a _____ of his car after it was stolen.

2. Fethi studied in France and the United States for many years. The _____ from his family was very difficult for him.

3. Professor Simons is a very _____ person. He has studied for twenty years in universities all over the world. He also speaks seven languages.

4. It will take some time for people to _____ working with robots.

5. Do you _____ that in the future robots will be a very common part of life?

6. Technology will make great _____ in the next century.

7. Silver is a very _____ metal. It is used in many important ways in society.

8. Modern society could not _____ without computers. They are everywhere today.

9. The art of early humans _____ many archaeologists. They search all over the world for new caves with paintings.

10. The Foreign Students Club is looking for a _____ for the office of president. The old president finished her studies and went back to her country last month.

B. Compound Words

A compound word is two smaller words put together. The meaning of the compound word is related to the meanings of the two words.

Here are some examples:

stop + light = stoplight (a light that makes cars stop)
note + book = notebook (a book to write notes in)

Make compound words by putting together a word from column A with a word from column B. Write the new compound words in column C.

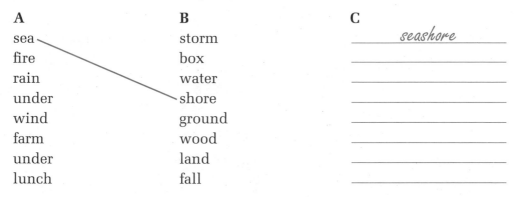

A	B	C
sea	storm	*seashore*
fire	box	
rain	water	
under	shore	
wind	ground	
farm	wood	
under	land	
lunch	fall	

Now choose the best new compound word from column C to complete each sentence.

1. Maria never buys food in the cafeteria. She prefers to bring a _____ with her own food every day.

2. We always keep a big supply of _____ to use in our fireplace in the winter.

3. The entrances to some caves are _____ or _____, so they are very difficult for scientists to find.

4. Last night there was a very bad _____. Many trees were blown over and fell into the streets. Traffic was terrible this morning because of all the fallen trees.

5. A desert is a very dry place to live. There is very little _____, so it's difficult to grow any kind of plants.

6. Parts of the United States are very beautiful. Some regions are mostly _____. You can see farms and animals everywhere. There aren't many big cities in these regions.

7. I would love to drive to the _____ this weekend. I like to drive along and look at the beautiful ocean. I think it's very relaxing.

C. Word Forms

This exercise is just for fun, and it is difficult. See if you can figure out the meanings of these words and use the correct word in each sentence.

unrecognizable	nonmechanized	undereducated	miscommunications
oversimplification	originality ✔	nonwarlike	complexities

1. An artist must have a lot of ____*originality*____. He or she must always think of new ideas.

2. Many people believe that wars begin because of hatred. This is an _____ of the problem. Wars begin for many complex reasons.

3. Developing countries have many problems. One problem is that most of the population is _____: The people need to learn more to make their country stronger.

4. Walking is a _____ method of transportation.

5. Switzerland is a _____ country. They usually remain neutral during wars, which means they don't join either side. They don't want to fight.

6. Tom wore a very strange costume to the Halloween party. His face was covered in makeup, and he was wearing a wig. He looked so different that he was completely _____.

7. When people learn a new language, they usually have a lot of funny stories to tell about different _____ that have happened.

8. We must recognize the difficulties and _____ of the problems in the world and work together to overcome them.

BUILDING VOCABULARY SKILLS

Vocabulary Review

Match the words in column A with their meanings in column B.

A	B
_____ 1. ancestors	a. groups
_____ 2. primitive	b. thin
_____ 3. tribes	c. reason
_____ 4. rare	d. money
_____ 5. bent	e. simple
_____ 6. purpose	f. notice
_____ 7. currency	g. uncommon
_____ 8. slender	h. not straight
_____ 9. worth	i. relatives
_____ 10. detect	j. value

Word List

The words focused on in the *Working with Vocabulary* activities are listed here. The number following each word indicates the <u>unit</u> in which the word is first introduced. Vocabulary items are recycled throughout the text.

A
abnormal 17
absorb 15
accurate 18
acronym 2
adapt 25
advance 23
advantage 25
advertisement 11
agreement 13
aisle 1
altitude 14
amateur 4
amount 1
ancestor 24
ancient 16
appear 10
appearance 23
archaeologist 16
area 8
arrange 7
artificial 8
assistance 19
athlete 4
attend 4
attractive 1
automatically 25
available 22

B
bark 22
beard 24
bent 23
berry 12
beverage 12
billboard 13
bitter 20
blend 12
blossom 12

blow 17
board 6
border 16
breathe 11
breathing 11
bury 7

C
calculate 10
carbon dioxide 15
cattle 9
cause 11
cave 16
celebrate 19
century 3
ceramic 21
chop down 22
clay 21
climate 13
coastal 15
coastline 9
code 7
coin 23
colony 8
combination 7
combine 13
communication 3
compare 23
compete 4
competition 4
competitor 4
complex 23
connect 2
consider 18
consume 20
container 1
continent 9
contribution 19
control 25

crack 21
create 15
currency 20
current 17
curve 16
customer 1

D
dairy 1
damage 17
decide 1
decorate 21
decrease 11
definite 18
degree 3
delicious 20
denim 5
describe 2
destination 12
detail 9
detect 14
developing 3
dial 2
digital 18
disabled 19
discover 9
disease 11
distant 9
distribute 23
divide 2
Dreaming 24
drip 18
dye 5

E
earn 6
effect 11
emergency 19
enable 18

encourage 15
enormous 22
entrance 16
equator 9
equipment 19
escape 15
event 4
even though 8
exactly 6
exhibit 7
exist 23
explorer 9

F
factory 5
fascinate 25
figure 18
forecast 14
fragile 21
fragrant 12
function 25
furniture 2

G
gambling 13
gather 20
generation 24
geography 9
glaze 21
glue 6
gold medal 4
grind 6
guide 14

H
habit 11
hammer 23
harbor 13
harmful 11

246

Index to the Word Study Activities

(248) 596-0067